Remembering Allah سبحانه وتعالى
Stories of the Chest & Heart
[Teenage Audience Adaptation]

❧ Medina House Publishing ❧

Cover Design: Medina House Publishing

Medina House
publishing

www.medinahouse.org
170 Manhattan Ave PO Box 63
Buffalo, New York 14215
contact@medinahouse.org

ISBN: 978-1-950979-12-7

Published in the United States of America

DEDICATION

Dedicated to all young adults in pursuit of truth

Table of Contents

ACKNOWLEDGMENTS

Many thanks to Dr. Yunus Kumek for granting us the
permission to adapt the original stories for a teenage audience

Preface

بِسْمِ اللّٰهِ الرَّحْمَنِ

الْحَمْدُ لِلّٰهِ رَبِّ الْعَالَمِينَ

اللهم صل عل سيدنا وحبيبنا ومولانا محمد

أَفَمَن شَرَحَ اللّٰهُ صَدْرَهُ لِلْإِسْلَامِ فَهُوَ عَلَى نُورٍ مِّن رَّبِّهِ فَوَيْلٌ لِّلْقَاسِيَةِ قُلُوبُهُم مِّن ذِكْرِ اللّٰهِ أُوْلَئِكَ فِي ضَلَالٍ مُّبِينٍ (الزمر / 22)

This book brings important lessons from the teachings of the Holy Quran, Sunnah and from the lives of the *Awliyaullah* (shortened forms: *Awliya* or *Wali*) into our everyday lives. *Awliyaullah* are the friends of Allah ﷻ. The term *Awliyaullah* is explicitly mentioned in the Quran when Allah ﷻ says:

أَلا إِنَّ أَوْلِيَاء اللّٰهِ لاَ خَوْفٌ عَلَيْهِمْ وَلاَ هُمْ يَحْزَنُونَ (يونس / 62)

{Unquestionably, [for] the allies/friends of Allah, there will be no fear concerning them, nor will they grieve.} (Yunus 10:62)

The stories in the book include interpretations and Discussion questions, and aim to use contemporary life encounters to convey Islamic teachings. The narratives expose the readers to important and practical aspects of Islamic teachings in our practical life. When there are referrals to Allah سبحانه وتعالى, then such words or phrases are capitalized (e.g. references such as the Divine). The abbreviation used for Prophet Muhammad ﷺ is the Prophet ﷺ.

The footnotes (with numbered superscripts) in each story provide the immediate relevant information for the unfamiliar English reader. Also, the endnotes (with lettered superscripts) provide information for readers who are familiar with the Islamic teachings and readings. The numbered references in parenthesis as superscripts provide literature references for claims made while discussing/interpreting the stories. The list of suggested readings are examples of some classical and contemporary works that are important references for further specialized readings. Finally, the Glossary and Index provided in the book can hopefully make the stories easily understood by general readers.

It is my fervent hope that the book would serve as a valuable tool for character building (especially among children and young adults) by presenting different perspectives in moral pedagogy combined with experiential religious and spiritual discourses of Islam.

Yunus Kumek, PhD

June, 2020.

1. A Fool's Filter

One Saturday afternoon, Sadr was reclining on the carpet of the mosque waiting for the prayer. As he sat there thinking about all his errands for the weekend, feelings of stress and anxiety began to overwhelm him. His state of mind became more aggravated with the entrance of a hunchbacked old man from the community named Nasreddin. Sadr did not know much about Nasreddin other than the fact that he was always in the mosque and was known to say strange things that no one else seemed to understand. Walking bowlegged as usual, he beelined straight to the back of the prayer space and into the mosque's kitchen space. Although the area is generally reserved for preparing meals during the mosque's events, this did not stop Nasreddin from rummaging through the cupboards only to come up with some ground coffee, sugar and a coffee maker. To Sadr's astonishment, he proceeded to place paper towels instead of the coffee filters into the machine. "What do you think you are doing?," Sadr yelled at the eccentric elder. "Making coffee", Nasreddin responded calmly. Sadr replied, "I know that". In frustration, he continued, "But why aren't you using the filters?" Nasreddin innocently asked, "If the coffee is the same, does it matter what filter you use?" "Yes, if it is not a proper filter you won't be able to make a proper cup of coffee" replied Sadr. "Then make sure you are using a proper filter", laughed Nasreddin as he exited the room. Sadr stood there dumfounded for a moment, then asked his Lord for

forgiveness for his lack of gratitude.

In practice...

In the story, Sadr did not approve of the paper towel being used as

a filter but later, found out the true meaning behind Nasreddin's actions.

He used the filter as a metaphor for Sadr's outlook on life. Because Sadr

was being pessimistic, it prevented him from properly evaluating his own

circumstances.

Discussion Question(s)

1. What is the importance of evaluating issues from another person's

    perspective?

2. The Humble Introvert

"He thinks he is better than us," Laith whispered to his friends as Yusuf walked by their group to sit in his usual spot in the library. Yusuf was known to eat his lunch alone every day at the same table next to the bookshelves. They had invited Yusuf to sit with them several times during the school year but he did not oblige them each time. Laith and the rest of the boys could think of no other reason other than his perceived arrogance. As Yusuf moved to sit down, he bumped into the shelf next to him which resulted in several books falling to the floor. The books clattered to the floor with the last few barely missing a classmate's table. Yusuf muffled an apology as he quickly rushed over to his assigned spot. Laith and the boys continued their conversation about Yusuf's lack of manners. "Clumsy Yusuf", Yusuf thought to himself, "This is exactly why you need to keep to yourself!"

In practice...

It is recommended to be in the company of righteous people. At the same time, being in the presence of Allah سبحانه وتعالى is considered a worthy virtue. Bastami, the great *wali* of Allah ﷺ says: "The true knower of Allah سبحانه وتعالى is the one who eats, drinks, jokes with you, sells to you, and buys from you, all while his heart is located in the kingdom of the Eternal Holiness [1]." Sometimes, it is difficult to maintain genuine

3

relationship with Allah سبحانه وتعالى and at the same time with people because there is always the possibility of breaking people's hearts, upsetting them, or even indulging in backbiting while in their company. Any potential harshness towards others can negatively affect one's genuine relationship with Allah سبحانه وتعالى. The Prophet ﷺ mentions that the real believer is the person from whom others are safe from his (her) hand and tongue [2]. There are Muslims who prefer solitude to minimize potentially negative engagements with others, although this may not be the widely accepted societal norm.

Discussion Question(s)

1. How can you stay humble while being involved in social interactions?

3. Enjoy the Ride

Ranya let out a sigh of relief as she exited her sedan and walked up the driveway to Dawla's house. She had just driven six hours from her campus in Albany, NY back to her hometown to visit her old school friend. When they met, Dawla asked Ranya about her trip. Ranya responded: "I thought it would be rough but luckily, I ended up using the drive time to complete my daily *Dhikr*." She continued: "It also didn't hurt that I had a few cups of cappuccino on the way", leading both friends to burst out laughing. Dawla silently wished that she was the one who had made the trip.

In practice...

Every moment we live through is an opportunity to improve and increase our relationship with Allah سبحانه وتعالى. A person is considered "unplugged" or disconnected from his (her) surroundings while driving. As such, traveling is one of the best means to refresh one's connection with Allah سبحانه وتعالى.

Discussion Question(s)

1. What are some of the things that prevent us from reflecting deeply?

4. An Orphan's Gift

One day, Tamer went home to play with his children. He saw that one of their friends was there as well. She was a 9-year-old Algerian orphan named Samira from the neighborhood. The orphan loved Tamer because he always gave her gifts each time he saw her. This time, Tamer had brought a large box of pastries from the local bakery. As the children rushed to get the delicacies, Tamer grabbed a doughnut and gave it to little Samira. As she ate the snack, Tamer patted her on the head affectionately. With a mouthful of doughnut, Samira said, "Thank you Uncle Tamer". Tamer smiled and replied, "I should be thanking you!"

In practice...

Orphans have a special status with Allah سبحانه وتعالى and they should be handled gently. Several verses of the Quran admonish against any harsh treatment of orphans. The Prophet ﷺ reminds us of the great reward for a person that comforts an orphan [3] . In the story, Tamer recognized that he benefited from gifting Samira, even more than she did from accepting the gift.

Discussion Question(s)

1. How do we prevent ourselves from being arrogant when helping others?

5. Experiential Learning

While Khaled was busy with his daily *Dhikr* in the living room, his brother Asad burst in angrily. He immediately started to list the challenges in his personal life. He spoke on everything: from his failing business to his unsuccessful quest to get married. All the while, Khaled listened quietly, without uttering a single word, other than the occasional *"SubhanAllah"* or *"Alhamdulilah"* amidst his brother's complaints. After a few minutes of absolutely no response from Khaled, Asad said: "You are my older brother! Why aren't you teaching me?" Khaled chuckled and calmly replied: "I am trying to!"

In practice...

Most of the time, it is very difficult to explain the peaceful states of *sakina* one experiences in the remembrance of Allah سبحانه وتعالى. Hence, some of the experts of the path assert that these teachings cannot be taught in a lecture format but should be experienced and lived through practice and worship.[i] [4]

Discussion Question(s)

1. How do we start learning from others' serene actions and state of being?

6. Spoiling the Honey

One day, Hafez attended a religious lecture. The people were angry, negative, and complained about their problems and the state of the Ummah. The meal served in that gathering was excellent, but the conversation was not. Hafez was disturbed by the lack of gratitude in a so-called religious gathering. He tried to enjoy his tea but somehow found that it just was not sweet enough. He continued adding honey to the cup but was still left unsatisfied. Finally, Hafez got up and proceeded to leave the gathering. "Where are you going?", one of the men yelled at Hafez, who was now near the door. "The honey is spoilt", replied Hafez, before finally exiting the conference hall.

In practice...

The relationship with Allah سبحانه وتعالى is like honey on the path[ii] of Islam. A person on the path is required to guard this valuable more than his (her) wealth because this is the real source of hope that makes the person continue striving on the path of Allah سبحانه وتعالى. Although the food in that gathering was excellent, Hafez was disturbed due to the negative influence on his spiritual state [5].

Discussion Question(s)

1. When you grow spiritually and morally, it is easy to lose your progress. How do you protect it?

7. Accepting Everyone at their Level

On a Friday evening, Malik sat with his four-year-old son, Muhammad, on his lap. They were engaged in a game on the living room sofa, whereby the little boy attempts to grab his father's beard, while the latter evades the former by moving his head at the last second. During their play, 16-year-old Ismail walked by, fiddling with his phone. Malik yelled at his distracted teenage son: "It might be wise that you take the trash out, considering that you promised to do it for the last two days and you are yet to do so". While the disgruntled Ismail stormed out to fulfill his promise, Muhammad finally caught his father's beard and tugged it hard. Malik screamed in pain. He then smiled and kissed his younger son's little fingers.

In practice...

Recognizing each person's situation: age, gender, culture, etc. in any interaction is very important. Failure to recognize this may cause injustice in social dealings. In the story, Malik was trying to imbibe this notion.

Discussion Question(s)

1. Is it always wise to treat everyone in the same way? Why or Why not?

8. Heavy Rain

One day, it was raining quite heavily. Darkness engulfed the entire skyline and intermittent thundering claps could also be heard. Dawud was busy enjoying the scenery of rain drops splashing against the concrete sidewalk outside his apartment. However, after some thoughts, he asked the Most Merciful for forgiveness and returned to his apartment to pray two *rakahs*.

In practice...

Rain can be a blessing or a problem. In history, some of the oppressive people or entire nations were punished with heavy rain, natural disasters, epidemics, or some other conditions by Allah سبحانه وتعالى. The Prophet Muhammad ﷺ used to like walking in rainy weather to receive its blessings [2]. At the same time, the Prophet ﷺ would immediately proceed to the mosque during any type of dark weather with heavy rain to ask forgiveness (for all humanity) from Allah سبحانه وتعالى, in case it was an indication of an impending punishment. Dawud upheld the Prophet's ﷺ *sunnah* in the story and he did not take any chance.

Discussion Question(s)

1. What other occurrences can either be a blessing or punishment in one's life?

9. Lean on Me

"*Allahu Akbar,*" proclaimed Kamal, as he folded his hands to begin another two units of prayer. Saturday after sunset was Kamal's set time of the week to engage in some extra supererogatory prayers. He began to recite the Quran, feeling his body relax, as he internally beseeched his Creator for guidance. As he continued through the prayer, he heard soft sobs from a corner of the mosque. After he finished his prayer, Kamal looked behind him to see what the issue was. He saw a young man of about 20 years old with his face in his hands, crying uncontrollably. Kamal walked over to the young man, but before he had completely closed the distance, he was hit with the strange and unfamiliar stench of alcohol. Kamal stopped in his tracks and questioned whether this was a situation he really wanted to get involved with. After all, he was now being forced to leave his worship. After some internal conflicts, Kamal reproached himself: "This is worship" and walked over to engage the young man.

In practice...

It is important to help people who are in need. Sometimes, a person can be in uncomfortable situations while helping others. Therefore, the intention and humility remain of paramount importance in maintaining piety. In the story, Kamal could have said, "I prefer worshiping Allah سبحانه وتعالى to helping this intoxicated and ungrateful young man", because

Muslims take enormous pleasure in their engagements with Allah سبحانه وتعالى. Rather, he considered helping others to be an integral part of worshipping the Creator.

Discussion Question(s)

1. How can you strike a balance between worship and service?

10. The Teenagers

Abdul Wali used to see some Muslim teenagers loitering the corners of the streets in his neighborhood. They were a "a bad crowd", as his dad observed, so he never used to associate with them. Nevertheless, he makes sure he extends Islamic greetings to this crew whenever he encountered them while on his way home from the mosque. Upon reaching home one evening, his mother asked him why he always greeted the young men. She said, "People might get the wrong impression and think that they are your friends and that you approve of them." Abdul Wali was bemused, and he responded, "I only wanted to fulfill their rights, but I will try to be more careful, *inshAllah*".

In practice...

It is very important to disengage oneself from any type of doubtful actions. In the story, as an exception, Abdul Wali greeted the wayward teenagers. In practice, it is important to know that ultimately, the real judgment will be made by Allah سبحانه وتعالى based on our intentions. Accordingly, a person will be rewarded or questioned about his (her) actions based on his (her) intentions.

Discussion Question(s)

1. Why is it important to disclose our intentions to people, if we only

    care about Allah سبحانه وتعالى؟

11. Reflection and *Dua*

One day, Maryam was pondering on the transience of life and the inevitability of death. She felt helpless. She was particularly scared because she did not know much about the details of the afterlife. Not knowing what else to do, she raised her hands to Allah سبحانه وتعالى in supplication and prayed that she should be safe from all the trials of death and the afterlife [6].

In practice...

Engagements and conversations with Allah سبحانه وتعالى through *dua* are very critical. In changing moments of life, *dua* can uphold a person and usher him or her from the darkness of hopelessness and fears into the light of hope and happiness. In the story, Maryam was in a self-critical engagement about life and death. As soon as she felt the unease of these unknowns, she immediately engaged herself in *dua*.

Discussion Question(s)

1. We all know the ephemeral nature of our earthly existence and the inevitability of our demise. Why do so many few people reflect on these known facts of life?

12. An Evil Haircut

Ali returned home after a long day at work. He placed his briefcase on the ground and took off his hat to reveal his grown hair, which was now almost shoulder length. When his wife saw him, she commented: "You need a haircut. You look like a barbarian!" Ali smiled and replied, "You watch too many movies." Then, he proceeded to change his clothes.

In practice...

There is no evil-looking person or being. Our interpretations of evil have largely been influenced by television, the internet, newspapers and even by events such as Halloween. With regards to this, Islam constantly urges spiritual cleansing through reflection and *Dhikr*.

Discussion Question(s)

1. Does Islam lay any emphasis on the physical appearance?

13. Look at a Pirate!

One morning, Safa was taking a leisurely walk with her kids. There was a man who seemed to be recovering from an eye surgery, wearing an eye patch, walking on the other side of the street. As the kids saw the man, they stared at him and told each other, "Look! there goes a pirate!" Safa was embarrassed and said to her children, "He is not a pirate. He only had an eye surgery. That is why one of his eyes is closed."

In practice...

It is important to deconstruct the impeded fabrications we learnt through childhood and adulthood about others, and more importantly about Allah سبحانه وتعالى. A wrong impression about people and Allah سبحانه وتعالى can be traced to an incorrect (and unfavorable) judgment of fellow humans or alienation from Allah سبحانه وتعالى. The children's' judgment of the man as a bad character is probably due to their exposure to popular culture [7]. Any wrong construction of Allah سبحانه وتعالى as a certain gender (male or female) with human qualities can alienate people from Allah سبحانه وتعالى because of any prior negative experiences or engagements with humans [8].

Discussion Question(s)

1. How can the media foster incorrect opinions about Allah سبحانه وتعالى and/or His religion?

14. The Lost Phone

One day, Asiya was on her way out of her home but could not find her phone. She checked her car. She checked her handbag. Yet, she could not find it. She was late for an important appointment. Asiya was interviewing graphic designers for an advertising position at her workplace. Using her husband's cell phone, she texted her own phone: "If you find this phone, please text me," and then, she left the house. As she drove to the café where she was meant to meet the prospective employees, Asiya began to try to rationalize the possible wisdom behind the inconvenience of losing her phone. Her heart told her there was some wisdom in the difficulty, but her mind could not comprehend what it could be. Three hours later, a person texted back that she had found the phone. After returning from the unproductive interviews, Asiya went to pick up the phone from the "good Samaritan's" house. Once she reached the location, she was greeted by a friendly older woman. After exchanging pleasantries with the lady and thanking her, she nonchalantly asked her what she did for a living. To her astonishment, the response was: "Graphic Design."

In practice...

Sometimes, people's immediate negative response to evil-appearing incidents can ruin their entire life. Patience, wisdom, and reflection should be practiced in all encounters of life [9].

Discussion Question(s)

1. Can you think of a situation in your life where an apparent bad

   situation eventually turned out good?

15. Religious People

One day, Omar was sitting in the local mosque and observing the board meeting. They were having a heated discussion on how to utilize the mosque's funds. Voices were raised, unsubstantiated claims were made, and rude fingers were pointed. Omar shook his head and aid, "*Alhamdulillah*, thanks to Allah سبحانه وتعالى, for saving me from the trial of leadership."

In practice...

It is very important to genuinely live what you practice. The purpose of *salah*, charity, fasting, and all other worship activities are to cleanse one's heart from spiritual diseases. If a person is becoming arrogant with religious affiliations, then this person is using the religion for his personal destruction on the path of Allah سبحانه وتعالى, regardless of his (her) position.

Discussion Question(s)

1. What dangers are there in leadership?

16. Smoked Salmon

Once Hind was told about the health benefits of salmon, she began to eat salmon...a lot. However, at a certain point, she began to develop a severe migraine whenever she ate the fish. She did not understand the reason for her ailment and proceeded to consult her doctor. The doctor informed her that although salmon is highly nutritious and full of immense health benefits, there was a lot of unnecessary salt in the smoked salmon she was consuming, and that the excess consumption was increasing her blood pressure. Hind was advised to adopt moderation in her food choice.

In practice...

It is very important to understand the general rules along with their applications under different circumstances. There can be a general rule related with a food item or an Islamic practice. Its application may differ from person to person, with its inherent benefits and harms. In the story, the smoked salmon is beneficial but only if taken in small quantities. Too much of it could pose a health problem. Similarly, we should strive for a balance in our Islamic practice: the applications depend on the context, time, and person.

Discussion Question(s)

1. How do Muslim scholars' religious advice vary with the context, time, and the individual's personal situation?

17. Out of my Hands

Huda sprung out of bed. As she remembered all the things that she needed to do that day, she grew a little apprehensive. She wished she could just stay at home but knew that was not a viable option. So, as usual, she started her day with her morning litanies. Her daily prayers offer her the necessary impetus to get through the day. She reminded herself, "I just need to do what needs to be done. If anything does not go the way that I desire, it is out of my hands."

In practice...

It is important to follow the reasons and means through the faculties of the mind, although one's heart (or spiritual faculties) may not feel inclined towards doing so. As believers, we should strive to let our minds dominate our hearts. When a person is accustomed to a secluded life of prayers without socializing with others, he (she) may feel secure due to the lack of human disturbances and mischief. Once such a person adopts a more social life and starts interacting with others, there are always possibilities of stress, oppression and evil. In spite of these possibilities, it is better to live a social life and be in the company of people and tolerate their vulgar proclivities, with the intention of rectifying their ways, while at the same time, living in a virtual space of union with Allah سبحانه وتعالى, through prayers, *Dhikr*, and reading the Quran and Hadith.

25

Discussion Question(s)

1. How do you prevent yourself from focusing on events, matters and

    outcomes outside your control?

18. All Dreams are Good Dreams

Basheer spent the entire morning in contemplation. He had abruptly woken up that morning, disturbed by an extremely vivid dream. Without getting into the details of the horrific nightmare, it suffices to say that he dreamt falling off a steep cliff after skipping his evening prayers. He craved more insights in interpreting the dream. After some thoughts and reflections, he decided it was a reminder from Allah سبحانه وتعالى for him to increase his acts of devotion. He then headed to the bathroom, to make ablution for prayer.

In practice...

In one of the sayings of the Prophet Muhammad ﷺ [10], Allah سبحانه وتعالى says, "I will treat My servant in the way he or she expects Me to be." Therefore, it is always important to have a good opinion of Allah سبحانه وتعالى. If we experience a bad dream, it is important not to publicize it, but to seek protection in Allah سبحانه وتعالى from the evils in the dream. Allah سبحانه وتعالى can do anything. Even if an evil has been ordained for a person, Allah سبحانه وتعالى can change the expected bad outcome into a positive one with His Divine Power.

Discussion Question(s)

1. What are some other ways that Allah سبحانه وتعالى can send us reminders?

19. Yesterday and Today

Mohsin thought about what he did the previous day. He reflected on what he had done that same day but a week prior. Then, he thought about what he had done so far today. He found that the three days were relatively the same. Mohsin began to weep.

In practice...

It is very important to eschew a stagnant spiritual life. We should avoid having similar consecutive days, without a positive change in our relationship with Allah سبحانه وتعالى. The Prophet ﷺ says, [11] "The person is not from us, if he (she) has the same day consecutively." In other words, every day is an opportunity to increase our knowledge, righteous practices, and closeness to Allah سبحانه وتعالى.

Discussion Question(s)

1. To progress on the path of spiritual reformation, do we have to be perfect at all times? Can we make mistakes and still progress?

20. Mowing the Lawn

Hassan pushed the lawnmower hard from one side of the lawn to the other. He was moving quickly as he was behind on his work schedule and needed to finish mowing the lawn as soon as possible. As he pushed the noisy machine, he suddenly spotted a small lizard darting through the grass. Quickly, he pulled back the machine handle, making it shudder and come to an abrupt stop. Once the lizard was at a safe distance, he restarted the machine and resumed his work.

In practice...

It is very important to respect all of creation. Size, worth and age do not matter. Life is given solely by Allah سبحانه وتعالى. One of the attributes of Allah سبحانه وتعالى is "The Alive,"[1] who gives and nurtures life. This is one of the attributes of Allah سبحانه وتعالى that Allah سبحانه وتعالى only manifests and the creation cannot replicate. If Allah سبحانه وتعالى gives life to any creature, we are expected to respect the creature's freedom of existence. The only exception is if such a creature poses a danger to us.

---

[1]   *Al-Hayy*

Discussion Question(s)

1. What are some of the ways that we inadvertently disrespect creation?

21. The Wound

While brushing his hair in the mirror, Sharif saw a small cut on his neck region, whose origin was unknown to him. He left the restroom in deep thoughts. Suddenly, he realized the plausible reason behind the wound. He immediately wept, prayed, and asked forgiveness from Allah سبحانه وتعالى. Then, he went back to the bathroom to get a bandage and disinfectant to dress his wound.

In practice...

Whatever happens to us has a reason. Nothing is random without any cause. There are external and internal meanings to everything. Some refer to this reality as destiny. In the story, before seeking medical intervention, Sharif immediately considered an internal possible reason for the wound that appeared on his body. Perhaps, his wound was due to his imperfect relationship with Allah سبحانه وتعالى. Hence, he prayed and asked forgiveness from Allah سبحانه وتعالى [12]. Afterwards, Sharif sought a medical intervention for his bodily injury.

Discussion Question(s)

1. What is the wisdom behind our personal sins bringing us worldly difficulties?

22. Cancer and the Unknown

After the doctors discovered a tumor in one of his father's lungs, Julaybib began to research Cancer as a terminal condition. He said to himself, "Why do people say that there is no cure for Cancer? What is the reason for its existence?" As he continued his research and pondered on the affliction, he could only come to one conclusion: "It is a signpost back to Allah سبحانه وتعالى."

In practice...

One of the attributes of Allah سبحانه وتعالى is "The Real Cause." Allah سبحانه وتعالى makes the means such as diseases to remind a person of his (her) limitations and the need for reliance on Allahسبحانه وتعالى. With the advent of scientific medical research and technological advancements, we often appear to be more independent and self-confident in our mortal abilities. The emergence of hitherto unknown severe diseases, comorbidities and epidemics could be a way of reminding and challenging humans about the need for Allah's سبحانه وتعالى help, protection and guidance.

Discussion Question(s)

1. What could Allah سبحانه وتعالى be teaching us through the emergence of diseases and epidemics?

2. What is the Islamic perspective on the Covid-19 corona virus epidemic?

3. Can less sophisticated creatures such as microscopic viruses and bacteria humble humanity?

23. The Cell Phone App and the Happy Old Man

There was an old man sitting in the mosque. Shuaib watched as the old man pulled out his cell phone and gleefully used a digital counter app to count his litanies. He seemed to be quite enthralled with the capability of his new app. After concluding his worship, he looked around the mosque and showed off the app to some of his friends. Apparently, he was proud of the "advanced technology" he had access to. "The digital counter!", he exclaimed in excitement. He failed to realize that the ubiquitous digital counter was an extremely old mobile phone application. Shuaib smiled and supplicated within himself, "May Allah سبحانه وتعالى protect us from the illusions of our own souls."

In practice...

In the path of Allah سبحانه وتعالى, we may think that we have attained very high ranks. Others with higher spiritual ranks and spiritual insights can easily identify this folly. We should always acknowledge the possibility that compared to others, we could be at lower spiritual levels on the path of Allah سبحانه وتعالى.

Discussion Question(s)

1. How do you shield yourself from believing you have attained a higher spiritual (or social) level than your actual status?

24. The Harsh Voice

In Abdul Kareem's communication with his class as a tutor, his loud voice would often catch his students off guard. However, this often had the desired effect of creating the disciplined atmosphere that he needed to facilitate his lessons. It allowed the students to fully comprehend the class lessons. After another long day at work, Abdul Kareem walked into his apartment. His expectant children rushed to meet him at the door. Abdul Kareem smiled and adjusted his voice to speak in the softest manner possible.

In practice...

It is very important to adapt our resources and actions to suit all situations. This includes our voices during communication with others. It is very vital we adopt a calm and reassuring disposition with our family members and friends. Likewise, depending on the situation, it may be appropriate to maintain a serious persona in public interactions, especially in business. Lowering our voice in communication as an Islamic teaching is prescribed in the verses of the Quran [49:2-4], the practices of the Prophet ﷺ and the lives of the *awliya* of Allah سبحانه وتعالى [13]. This teaching can help us attain genuine traits of mercy and care towards all the entire creation of Allah سبحانه وتعالى.

Discussion Question(s)

1. What are situations where a teacher needs to be "soft" with his (her) students?

2. Can there be any circumstance where a parent needs to be "hard" with his (her) children?

25. Oppression and Friends

Amina visited her friends on Monday night. She was very excited to see them all. They shared a delicious meal and chatted late into the night. After a while, Amina left her companions and went home to bed. However, she was unable to sleep. The next day, she still felt uneasy and tried to figure out what could be the issue. Finally, she murmured to herself, "My arrogance!"

In practice...

Islam regards all good achievements attained by humans as blessings from Allah سبحانه وتعالى. On the other hand, all evils afflicting us are attributed to our ill actions. Therefore, we should always be in a state of gratitude to Allah سبحانه وتعالى whenever we experience any good fortune. Likewise, we should exercise patience, rely solely on the Creator, and seek His forgiveness whenever we are subjected to any misfortune. If make any sole claim on any accomplishment, then we will be lying and oppressing ourselves. We should be wary of such assertions as they can adversely affect our spirituality and derail us from a path of moral reformation.

Discussion Question(s)

1. What is the difference between confidence and arrogance? Does there exist a thin line between the two traits?

26. Night Life

During the summers, Saeed would usually sleep late at night. He found that no matter how much he slept; he still felt tired. Moreover, his days seemed to pass fleetingly, and he got very little done. Afterwards, he decided to change his routine and he quickly realized positive changes in his life. As before, he was awake for the same period but was now far more productive. He now understood the true meaning of *baraka*.

In practice...

In accordance with some of the prophetic narrations, it is advisable to avoid conversations or any engagements after the last prayer of the day [10] [2]. Most humans are less productive during these periods due to hormonal changes and our mortal needs for sleep. Moreover, Islam believes unseen creatures of the Creator are known to be active during these periods as *Rasulullah* ﷺ clearly indicated in some of the authentic Hadiths. Indeed, there is more *baraka* in our time during the day.

Discussion Question(s)

1. Why is staying up late at night bad for you? What are some of the detrimental effects on the human health?

2. Are some other people more productive during the nighttime?

27. Spiritual Poverty

There was a poor man who frequented the mosque. He smelled bad, looked dirty and was very crude in his speech. No one wanted to associate with him. During the evening prayer, he stepped into the prayer line, right next to Abdullah. To Abdullah's chagrin, the destitute man inadvertently pressed his rough shoulder against his. As Abdullah tried to maintain concentration in his prayers and ignore the unpalatable odor oozing off his companion's body, he suddenly saw some little drops of liquid hit the praying mat. To his surprise, he realized that the poor man was silently weeping due to the Imam's recitations. Abdulla felt a surge of guilt rise in his heart and he asked Allah سبحانه وتعالى to forgive him.

In practice...

As believers, we should never judge people based on their looks, clothing, race, culture, or any social/demographic identifier. Several prophetic teachings have asserted that seemingly shabby or ill-dressed people could have surprisingly very high spiritual levels before Allah سبحانه وتعالى [2]. It is also very important to have good opinions or thoughts about fellow humans.

Discussion Question(s)

1. How do we train ourselves to focus less on peoples' outward

   appearances?

28. The Fly Catcher

The neighborhood mosque had big windows that always stayed closed. Flies often entered the mosque through the doors but get trapped inside, flying against the windowpanes, and trying to escape. Before sunset on most days, Nusaibah is often seen, gently collecting the flies with paper towels, without hurting them and placing the little creatures back outside. She would feel great pleasure and satisfaction as she saw each fly regain its freedom, flying outside freely. For each fly that she released, she used to say "*Alhamdulillah*, {thank you Allah سبحانه وتعالى}" 33 times, to appreciate Allah سبحانه وتعالى for giving her the ability to accomplish a good deed.

In practice...

All creatures are precious and should be respected. It is highly meritorious to preserve a life, irrespective of its size or usefulness. Like Nusaibah, it is important to recognize that the ability to execute a good deed is from Allah سبحانه وتعالى. Perhaps, Nusaibah preferred to execute this good deed before sunset because this time amplifies one's good deeds. Each day, angels present our deeds during the daytime to Allah سبحانه وتعالى before sunset, while our night deeds are presented after sunrise [10].

Discussion Question(s)

1. Why does Nusaibah value something as small as a fly?

29. Two Prayers

It was time for the annual Eid prayers[2]. People were in dispute about the actual date of the Eid prayer due to disagreements on moon sighting among the local scholars. Each person had a position that was largely influenced by one of the two mosques in the community that he (she) regularly attended. Quarrels seem to pervade the entire Muslim community based on this divergence of opinion. Warda observed this dispute in her community from afar and smiled to herself. She said, "*Alhamdulillah*, {thanks to Allah سبحانه وتعالى}, there is a difference in opinion about the date of the annual prayers for this year. I can attend Eid on two different days in two different venues!"

In practice...

Praying to Allah سبحانه وتعالى is not a burden but a sweet desired engagement with the Creator. If we find different opportunities of fostering a relationship with our Creator, then we should seize such opportunities to derive sweetness in our relationship with Allah سبحانه وتعالى.

---

[2]   Eid prayer

Discussion Question(s)

1. How do we reconcile differences between different Islamic groups,

    scholars, or mosques?

30. Lifestyle Changes

When Azhar was a farmer in his homeland of Egypt, he enjoyed consuming huge servings of meat-based meals. Then, he migrated to North America, became a writer, and now spends most of his time behind a desk. However, he still favored eating a lot of meat and its derivatives. He loves his new home country and occupation, but he often finds himself falling ill. His friend, who is a vegetarian was worried about Azhar's health. He advised him, "You really need to change your eating habits. You are no longer a farmer; you need to adjust your diet accordingly!"

In practice...

It is important to understand our own personal situation and circumstances. This includes watching what we eat. As our lifestyles change, we need to adapt our eating habits to suit our new situation. To excel spiritually, we may need to embrace healthier eating habits.

Discussion Question(s)

1. How does our diet affect our spirituality?

31. Junk Food Judgments

Abdul Wahid loved hanging out with his classmates on the weekends. At these gatherings, his friends would eat Burgers and French fries, and drink ice cold sodas. As Abdul Wahid was very health-conscious, he would frown at his friends' meal choices, refrain from eating the unhealthy meals and wonder, "How can we consume unhealthy meals and still remain good Muslims?" One day, Abdul Wahid was very hungry but did not have a single morsel of food in his apartment. Luckily, a friend happened to be in his neighborhood and decided to pay Abdul Wahid a visit. The friend came along with some French fries, deep-fried pastries, soda cans, and several unhealthy cookies. Abdul Wahid thought to himself, "I am so hungry, I will eat some of these!" He then proceeded to eat. Afterwards, he felt some guilt for flouting his healthy eating habits, but he now had some sympathy for his classmates.

In practice...

It is highly recommended to only eat healthy meals so we can maintain a healthy physical and spiritual relationship with Allah سبحانه وتعالى. However, depending on our circumstances, we may partake in other meals if they are lawful. This is especially relevant if we are invited as guests to an event or occasion, then we are expected to eat whatever meal is provided.

We should only decline such a meal, without offending the hosts, if it is unlawful or extremely dangerous to our health.

. Discussion Question(s)

1. How do you maintain discipline without judging others?

32. Good Opinions

It was a bright sunny Friday afternoon and as usual, Leena attended the local mosque for the congregational prayer. Everyone seemed to be very happy. Before commencement of the homily, smiles, hugs, kisses, and pleasantries were being exchanged throughout the mosque's parking lot and entrance areas. Although Leena was somewhat shy, she greeted everyone she met both before and after the prayer. As she exited the building afterwards, she saw two sisters walking alone. Unlike others in the mosque, the sisters appeared very upset and gloomy. She really was unaware of their situation, but she thought to herself, "Indeed, it is the practice of *Rasulullah* ﷺ to always smile and adorn a cheerful disposition." She failed to embrace a good opinion about these sisters and went home without greeting them. Later, she returned to the mosque for the evening prayer and observed the presence of several people for a funeral prayer. The same sisters she encountered earlier during the day were also there and the deceased was their father! Leena now understood the reason behind their misery and admonished herself for inadvertently making an ill-formed judgment about others.

In practice...

There are always exceptions to all general rules and teachings. As humans, losing a loved one is a painful and harrowing experience. Having a genuine empathy for the bereaved is a virtue and Allah سبحانه وتعالى rewards people who have sympathy for those with broken hearts due to a loss or hardship. Grief or any other life circumstance could make us exhibit untoward and transient "out-of-character" behavior or attitude. Thus, we should hesitate before judging others.

Discussion Question(s)

1. Do people jump to conclusions when they see something out of place? Why?

33. Teaching your Own

Badriyya spent her weekdays enduring the commotion of a fourth grader classroom at the elementary school she taught. At the end of such days, she will return to her family and her own kids. When she returns home, she will often get annoyed with her own children. One day, she thought to herself, "How should I change my perspective so that I don't get annoyed with my own kids?" After much thoughts and contemplations, she replied herself, "If I consider them as my students and parenting as my job, then perhaps I will see everything as normal!"

In practice...

It is important to raise our children on the path of Allah سبحانه وتعالى. In practice, most teachers and scholars raise and train their own children just as they teach their students [14]. It is a grave mistake if one becomes a teacher for others, but not for one's immediate kinship groups.

Discussion Question(s)

1. Why do some teachers neglect their own children?

34. Wishing for a Sandwich

Julaybib longed for a sandwich. But the bread was in the bread cabinet; the spices were high up in the food rack; the Cheese, Pickles, Mayo, and the Lettuce were still in the fridge. In addition, the utensils he needed to prepare the meal were still in the top drawer. Making a meal is simply a lot of work to do on a lazy afternoon. Julaybib smiled to himself, raised his hands and made the supplication: "Allah, kindly grant me the highest level of Heaven."

In practice...

Patience and struggle are needed to achieve the worldly pleasures of life. If we decide to embark on a travel for vacation, we should be prepared to endure travelling inconveniences with patience till we arrive our destination. Likewise, patience and self-struggle would serve us on our path towards spiritual reformation; and ultimately, Allah سبحانه وتعالى promises us Heavenly pleasures in the afterlife devoid of any more struggle or effort. Julaybib's earthly desire made him yearn for the effortless pleasures that abound in Paradise.

Discussion Question(s)

1. Why are worldly or spiritual achievements associated with struggles?

35. The Scholar and Baklawa

There was once a visiting female scholar in the local Islamic center. During a community event, she was served baklawa. She took a piece of the delicious pastries and returned it back to the plate without eating it. Then, she licked her fingers. "What are you doing?", her bewildered female students asked. "Training," smiled the shaykha.

In practice...

It is highly meritorious to keep the company of genuine scholars and learn from them. Most beneficial learning occurs when a student or disciple spend time with his (her) teachers and scholars during the course of normal daily activities [16]. The genuine scholar is an embodiment of his (her) teachings. In the story, the teacher probably uses self-restraint for her own self-discipline. She did not totally shun the delicacy, even though she knew that her ego greatly desired it. Rather, she permitted her ego a slight reprieve by licking her fingers to mildly taste the food. Recognizing our desires and needs of the self (ego) will help us to train it.

Discussion Question(s)

1. What is the importance of controlling your desires?

36. The Inside is What Counts

There was a radiologist in private medical practice that would often return home with his work files. While awaiting his dinner in the living room, he would continue working while his wife prepares the evening meal. His wife would usually see the digital images of his patients' different internal organs, such as livers, kidneys, gall bladders, etc. Each time she sees these images, she would feel some disgust. One evening, while setting the family dinner on the dining table, she again saw these images and wondered, "Why are people physically attracted to one other?". She continued in her thoughts, "Our 'insides' are all the same!"

In practice...

It is important to recognize that outward manifestations may mean little. Although Allah سبحانه وتعالى created all humans perfect and beautiful, what really matter are the internal manifestations of piety, love, respect, and appreciation for Allah سبحانه وتعالى. This is known as *taqwa*. This concept is greatly emphasized in the Quran and Hadith. The Prophet ﷺ says, "Allah سبحانه وتعالى does not value your physical appearances, but values what is in your hearts and actions [2]," and a popular verse of the Quran mentions that Allah سبحانه وتعالى created (us with) different ethnicities and genders to know one another so that we can maximize *taqwa* with the opportunities of

diverse interactions[iii].

Discussion Question(s)

1. As humans, why do we focus less on our internal manifestations?

37. A Dark Monday

Hodan woke up on a dark Monday morning. Looking outside through her curtained windows, she immediately felt despondent and experienced a longing to move elsewhere. But she could not, because she needed to go to work throughout the entire week. On reflection, she became disappointed in herself because she felt ungrateful to her Creator. She thought to herself, "Fasting should do the trick!"

In practice...

We can change our world outlook and perspective in life by fasting. In Islam, Fasting entails abstaining from food, drink, and other lawful acts (such as intercourse with a spouse) from sunrise to sunset. As recommended by *Rasulullah* ﷺ, fasting on Mondays and Thursdays can encourage self-discipline. Fasting, as an act of worship, allows us to enrich our mental faculties, mind, body, and soul. By depriving ourselves of lawful necessities of life, we become grateful to the Creator for bestowing us with such privileges.

Discussion Question(s)

1. How can excessive eating and drinking adversely affect our spirituality?

38. What a Deal!

While driving back home, Shefa saw a store with a bright neon display that flashed, "Going out of Business Sale". She sparked her car in the store's parking lot and entered the store. Before long, she already bought a few dozen items. An item with a list price of $30.00 was sold for only a few dollars. Beaming with joy over the great deals in her cart, she proceeded to make her payments. She planned to share the news with her friends and family. Suddenly, she stopped in her strides and thought about the plight of the store owner. She felt sad that the owner's business was going through a bankruptcy. She muttered to herself, "It is so sad. Glory be to the Owner who gives much without losing."

In practice...

It is very important to express our sympathy towards others when they experience a loss or calamity. If we benefit from others' misfortune, then this is not a real gain. Our sincerity towards others dictates that we should desire good for our fellow humans. Without measure, Allah سبحانه وتعالى, as the Real Owner, can honor us with very precious gifts in this life and in the afterlife for very little efforts on our part. All His numerous favors towards us neither diminishes His bounties nor cause him any loss.

Discussion Question(s)

1. Could Shefa have done anything to assist the owner? What could
   she have done different?

39. Sleep is the Cousin of Death

Guled fell asleep on the carpet in the mosque after the Morning prayer. He was tired and tried to fall asleep, but he only succeeded to be semi-conscious: He was in slumber and yet, he was still aware of the noises around him. He tried to rouse himself from sleep, but he could not. He could neither move his torso nor any of his limbs. In his state, he thought, "Now I understand what death is like. The body dies but not the soul."

In practice...

Death is all around us. Our eventual demise is a reality we cannot evade. When we die, our physical body dies, but our soul subsists. The body is no longer under the command of the soul. There are some narrations from *Rasulullah* ﷺ that indicates buried dead people can hear humans in close proximity to their graves [2]. Guled was in the state of half sleep and half wakefulness. There is a special name for this state[3] in Islamic theology. In this state, he rationalized the relationship between the soul and body through his own personal experience. Just as Guled submitted in the story, the Quran also mentioned that the sleeping state is akin to death[iv].

---

[3] *Yaqaza means the mixed state of sleep and awareness.*

Discussion Question(s)

1. If not being able to wake up reminds us of death, what does

    "waking up" reminds us of?

40. Regrets

There was a Muslim man who frequently loses his temper when subjected to difficult situations. After each loss of temper, he will regret his actions and reproach himself, "I wish I was patient enough, I wish I didn't utter those awful words, I wish I didn't talk too much... I wish... I wish..."

In practice...

In all situations, we must endeavor to control ourselves and when we fail to do so, we should seek forgiveness from Allah سبحانه وتعالى and pray for self-restraint. *Rasulullah* ﷺ was once asked who the most powerful person was. Everyone present in the gathering thought it was a strong person who could defeat his enemies in an altercation or battle. The Prophet ﷺ replied, "No, it is the person who can control his (her) anger" [10].

Discussion Question(s)

1. What is the difference between controlling your anger when you are in a position of power and when you are not?

41. Accepting Criticism

Dariya finished writing the draft manuscript of her first book. She sought feedback from her friends, colleagues, and family. Everyone she approached provided with advice and tips on how to improve the book's quality. Her intimate friend, Rufaidah also obliged her and offered her similar advice. Dariya thought everyone was envious of her achievement and that they were all criticizing her work unnecessarily. Rufaidah said to her, "Dear friend, if everyone is providing you with similar comments about your book, then you should really stop seeing them as adversaries and appreciate their efforts." In reflection, Dariya lowered her head in shame.

In practice...

Creating imaginary adversaries only increases our own arrogance and insecurities. We should be able to handle all criticisms and strive to use such critiques to perfect our craft or endeavors. It is important to improve ourselves through others, even if they may have insincere intentions or motives when giving us advice. Jealousy is a reality of our human existence. In such cases, litanies and prayers suffice to protect us from all evil machinations of envious people.

Discussion Question(s)

1. Why it is more difficult to accept criticism from some people than from others? If possible, explain with examples from your personal experiences.

42. Bad Company

Sami asked his friend for advice about helping a person in need. His friend suggested some ways of helping, but the suggestions were either unethical or dishonest. Sami felt uneasy about the recommendations and failed to act on them. However, his friend kept insisting that there was nothing wrong if the outcome was guaranteed to be good. Sami did not relent in his decision, and their arguments continued back and forth, without any discernable action.

In practice...

It is important to reach a virtuous act through virtuous and ethical measures. We gain support from Allah سبحانه وتعالى for being honest and just in our affairs. Adopting high ethical standards can help secure reward in this world and in the afterlife. Verily, a true honest person may not be appreciated by his peers, friends, or family members, but Allah سبحانه وتعالى is truly pleased with such an individual.

Discussion Question(s)

1. How do you deal with a friend that urges you to indulge in a wrong or commit a misdeed?

43. Spiritual Treats

Anas's wife would buy boxes of nutritious snacks for her children to take to school. The snacks were wholesome, healthy, and organic. However, they were quite expensive. His wife would place the snacks in the pantry, making them easily accessible to the kids. Anas would often overhear his wife chiding the kids for eating all the snacks at home, without leaving any for the next day's lunch bags. He would listen to her and smile, "The snacks are there. Why wouldn't the kids eat them?"

In practice...

Spiritual treats are granted by Allah سبحانه وتعالى as an encouragement for the traveler on the journey [17]. As humans, if we have unbridled access to such spiritual treats, our natural inclination will be to grab them all entirely. All blessings, honors and favors are provided and controlled by Allah سبحانه وتعالى. Unless empowered by Allah سبحانه وتعالى, we have no control over them. This is even true for the Prophet ﷺ. All prophets and messengers only performed miracles or other supernatural feats with Allah's سبحانه وتعالى permission and empowerment.

Discussion Question(s)

1   How can we ensure we only worship Allah سبحانه وتعالى sincerely for His sake?

44. Nightly Visitations

An old man would often visit the bathroom before going to bed each night. He believed failure to do so will discomfort his body organs and ruin all the balance they worked hard to achieve during the day. Even if he did not feel the urge to relieve himself on some nights, he will still proceed to the bathroom before sleeping. One cold night, he was so tired that he slept without this nightly routine. The next day, he woke up in distress, feeling some pains in his abdomen. He believed the pains emanated from his kidneys and bladder. He thought to himself, "I did not fulfill their rights."

In practice...

The human body parts may complain in this life and in the afterlife. In the story, the old man was wary of not fulfilling the needs of his internal body organs. The Noble Quran[v] mentions that some of our body parts will serve as witnesses to our earthly actions.

Discussion Question(s)

1. Can our body parts serve as witnesses against us on the Day of Judgment? Will they have complaints against us? If so, what could be their likely grievances?

45. Soft Spoken

Safiyyah finally realized that her family and friends had some reservations about her loud, intimidating voice. She now makes a conscious effort to lower the intensity of her voice in all her conversations. Consequently, this made most people to be more comfortable in her presence. One Sunday evening, she was engaged in a debate with her friend and unintentionally raised her voice. She glanced at her friend's face and realized that the latter seemed intimidated. Immediately, Safiyyah modified her voice and continued with her arguments. Her friend smiled and nodded in agreement. Subconsciously, Safiyyah joined her friend in laughter.

In practice...

It is considered a virtue to control our voice and emotions when engaged in discussions with others. This becomes more paramount when we are interacting with fellow spiritual travelers, teachers, or parents. In fact, the Noble Quran[vi] instructed the companions of *Rasulullah* ﷺ to lower their voices in their communications with him.

Discussion Question(s)

1. Are people influenced by the way we present our advice(s) to them? If so, give some examples from your personal experience.

46. Self-Struggle is the Goal

Bilal woke up this morning with a game plan. He planned to eat a hearty breakfast so he would not be tempted to snack on unhealthy pastries throughout the day. He intended to take a short nap after lunch to prevent excessive laziness during the latter part of the day. He planned to communicate clearly with his coworkers to prevent future quarrels. To avoid procrastination, he intended to recite some verses of the Quran immediately he arrived home from work. He had clear objectives, and he prepared to achieve them all.

In practice...

The goal of threading the path of spiritual reformation is "Self–struggle"[4]. This goal is neither a physical exertion of our bodies, nor the exercise of our intellectual prowess. Rather, it is an internal struggle and control to seek the pleasure of Allah سبحانه وتعالى. The Noble Quran says that Prophet Abraham met Allah سبحانه وتعالى with a tranquil heart, free from spiritual diseases[5]. Likewise, *Rasulullah* ﷺ also reminded his companions that the physical struggle [such as battles in the cause of Allah

---

[4]   *Jihad*

[5]   Qalbun Saliim.

سبحانه وتعالى] was only a minor one when compared to the internal struggle of the self [10] [2].

Discussion Question(s)

1. How do you avoid getting overwhelmed in your self-struggle?

47. The Worried Muslim

Maliha worries about the future. She has no idea where she would be in a decade from now, and that reality really scares her. "I will be honest, I won't oppress anyone or myself, I won't break anyone's heart, I won't waste my time, I will exercise patience and embrace complete reliance in Allah سبحانه وتعالى." After making these promises today, she felt good and thought to herself, "Whatever comes my way will be in my best interest."

In practice...

Every day is a new opportunity with unknowns, both good and bad. Islam teaches that our actions will be adjudged by our intentions. Without an insight to the future, Maliha made intentions to accomplish some good deeds. If, for whatever reasons, she is unable to fulfil her promises, Allah سبحانه وتعالى will still reward her because she had good intentions. Muslims are encouraged to do their very best in any endeavor without over-burdening themselves. Thereafter, they are enjoined to fully rely on Allah سبحانه وتعالى [18]. This is referred to as *tawakkul* in Islamic theology.

Discussion Question(s)

1. Making plans is a teaching of Islam. How do you avoid an over-reliance on your plans?

48. The Intellectuals

Serene attended a gathering of highly educated Muslims to discuss various societal issues along with Islam. Serene opined, "Islam cannot be discussed like the other social sciences. We need to adopt humility in both our attitudes and language, even if we have divergent opinions." Most attendees seemed offended by her opinion, and one of the more vocal men in the gathering replied her, "We are intellectuals. We can discuss anything and everything without restrictions or boundaries. Your convoluted opinion is precisely the reason why religion has lost its relevance and it simply does not conform to the modern approaches!" Serene wanted to respond to the man's vitriol, but she thought better of it. Rather, she kept quiet and found the earliest excuse to exit the gathering.

In practice...

The religious sciences cannot be addressed like other disciplines. This is of greater importance if the knowledge of Allah سبحانه وتعالى is the topic of discourse. At all times, we must ensure we have proper *adab* of words, thoughts, and actions. Doing this enables us to learn effectively and improve spiritually.

Also, a Muslim's silent moments should be filled with deep reflections on Allah سبحانه وتعالى. Our eloquence and intellects are of little significance on the path of spiritual redemption. Rather, having the proper *adab* with Allah

سبحانه وتعالى, and others is more important. Indeed, our words should be pearls that deeply penetrates the hearts our fellow humans.

Discussion Question(s)

1. What does it really mean to be an intellectual?

49. The Cool Car

Zainab now drives a used sports car that her older sister just gave her. Her kids believe their mother now owns the coolest car in the neighborhood. During today's ride to the mall, her oldest son said to her, "Mom, you have such a nice car. Your friend, Umm Imran's car is nothing comparable to yours!" Zainab smiled to herself, "If he only knew the worth of this car in comparison to my friend's, he would be so disappointed!"

In practice...

In our relationship with Allah سبحانه وتعالى, others may have a very high opinion about us. They may see us as an *awliya,* saint or friend of Allah سبحانه وتعالى. We should be wary of this as focusing on false appearance can lead to lies and arrogance. *Rasulullah* ﷺ often makes a *du'a,* "Oh Allah! Please, elevate my status in the eyes of people and lower my status in my own eyes [19]." *Rasulullah* ﷺ sought an elevated status from people because he wanted them to respect and listen to Allah's سبحانه وتعالى message. On the other hand, *Rasulullah* ﷺ teaches us to avoid arrogance by underestimating our own self-worth".

Discussion Question(s)

1. Why do we tend to exaggerate praises for our loved ones?

50. Texting and Driving

Hamza would often witness strange incidents in his daily commute to work. One morning, he saw a driver in the next lane that was texting on her mobile phone while driving. She was so engrossed with the phone that she almost collided with another vehicle. Luckily for her, she was finally able to bring her vehicle to a halt before any collision. Hamza observed her looking pale, stressed and quite shaken due to the incident. He smiled and said aloud to himself, "I don't understand why folks subject themselves to unnecessary stress. What a wasted opportunity!"

In practice...

Every situation is an opportunity to improve our relationship with Allah سبحانه وتعالى. A focused Muslim driver while enjoying the beauty of nature and the usual solitude of driving alone, can also engage in *dhikr* to alleviate his (her) fears, stress, and anxieties. In the story, the driver subjected herself to a stressful situation by engaging in an inappropriate and unsafe behavior. She failed to use the opportunity to communicate directly with her Creator.

Discussion Question(s)

1. Despite the inherent danger associated with texting and driving, why do some people still engage in such a dangerous act?

73

51. Ice Cream on Me

Lana and her friend Ayan took their kids out for ice cream. As the kids ordered their choices of flavor and topping, Ayan got a little apprehensive as she realized how much the entire order was going to cost. Even though she had enough money with her, she did not want to pay for the entire bill and planned to tell the cashier to split the bill between her and her friend. Lana approached the cashier, paid for the entire order, and whispered to her friend, "It's all on me!"

In practice...

Generosity is a virtuous trait. Allah سبحانه وتعالى gives to us without measure. We are only required to recognize and appreciate His blessings. In the story, Ayan probably suffers from a spiritual sickness of stinginess and a fear of spending on others. Her friend's generous action will likely make her understand the folly of her stinginess.

Discussion Question(s)

1. What are some practical ways of combating stinginess?

52. Count your Blessings

Sara was upset with her classmates because they failed to show gratitude to all their teachers. They constantly discussed and exaggerated each instructor's minor faults. She thought to herself, "I just can't comprehend this. You have benefited tremendously from your teacher. Now, when you observe his (her) trivial faults, then you become ungrateful and claim you haven't benefited from him(her)."

In practice...

Islam teaches that people that we benefit from have rights over us. Foremost, we are expected to show gratitude to Allah سبحانه وتعالى, followed by our parents and then, our teachers. It is unethical when we fail to recognize and appreciate the benefits we receive from our teachers.

Discussion Question(s)

1. Why do people usually show less gratitude to those close to them?

53. Lessons from Balding

Yahya used to keep his hair short. He lacked the patience and time to maintain a long hair. The effort was simply too much for him and he clearly acknowledged that keeping a long hair will be a messy affair for him. He never understood how a man could keep a long hair and would often mock his brother for his signature ponytail. One morning, he looked in the mirror. He realized he was losing his hair and that some sections of his head had already become bald. To avoid further hair loss, he decided to avoid shaving or cutting his hair anymore. After a year, he realized he was now fully bald. Suddenly, having a ponytail did not seem all that bad.

In practice...

It is important to appreciate all the favors from Allah سبحانه وتعالى. The first favor is good health. Other important favors are knowing Allah سبحانه وتعالى and having the ability to worship Him. Our intellects, physical strengths, ability to eat, ability to breathe without support, etc. are also some of the numerous favors from our Lord. When we become ill or lose some of these abilities, we tend to get envious of those who still possess them. Once we realize we may lose some of the Creator's favors, we should grasp and hold them tight. Thus, the spiritual states of *hamd*, *shukr*, and sincere appreciations are very important in the life of a believer. Allah سبحانه وتعالى accords Prophet Muhammad ﷺ a high status because he constantly showed appreciation and *hamd* to Allah سبحانه وتعالى. In fact, the name or title "Muhammad" refers to the one who always appreciates and is thankful to Allah سبحانه وتعالى.

Discussion Question(s)

1. Why should be avoid judging others, especially when we are not privy to their backgrounds or motivations?

54. The Headache

One day, Amatullah woke up with a severe headache. She was in severe pains and wondered about the cause of her discomfort. She avoided taking any medications until she performed some *Dhikr* for spiritual healing. She went to the bathroom to make ablution[6]. Then, she prayed and felt a little better, but she still felt some soreness. She began reading some verses from the last three chapters of the Holy Quran. After reading thrice, she blew on her hands and rubbed her body with her hands as *Rasulullah* ﷺ recommended [20]. She felt even better but still felt traces of the headache. She wondered if it was time to take a painkiller pill or should she continue to bear her pains? After some deliberations, she decided to recite some Prophetic prayers for illness. Then, she went to sleep, while supplicating for a cure. She woke up feeling much better and smiled, "*Alhamdulillah*, thanks to Allah سبحانه وتعالى, I didn't need any medication."

In practice...

We should consult Allah سبحانه وتعالى on any issue or problem before seeking assistance through other alternate means. These alternate means can only benefit us if Allah سبحانه وتعالى empowers them. In the

---

[6]   *Wudhu*

story, the pill is an alternative solution for headache. Amatuallah's supplications, readings from the Quran [21] and litanies of *Rasulullah* ﷺ sufficed to alleviate her ailment. However, if these failed to ease her pains, she could have taken the medication and ask Allah سبحانه وتعالى to make the pills a sufficient remedy.

Discussion Question(s)

1. What is (are) the wisdom(s) behind Allah's سبحانه وتعالى creation of the 'means', when He does not need them?

55. Humble Beginnings

There was a small wooden table in a corner of the mosque. Congregants in the mosque would usually place the garbage can on this table. One day, Reem was searching for a table to place her copy of the Holy Quran so she could comfortably read some passages. Apart from the plastic tables, there were no available tables within reach. As Reem always preferred natural pieces, she looked around and saw the wooden table with a garbage can on it. She smiled and thought, "Now, your status will be elevated and noble, *inshAllah*." She cleared, thoroughly cleaned, and perfumed the table. Then, she placed the Quran on it to read. After a few months, this wooden table became the most preferred table in the mosque for reading the Quran. No one wanted to use the other plastic tables. One day, Reem entered the mosque and saw two people quarrelling over the table. She viewed the scene and said, "Allah سبحانه وتعالى elevates and He abases."

In practice...

Most times, we fail to consider others' pasts before criticizing them. Despite being on the path to Allah سبحانه وتعالى, anyone can have a bad history. Even the selected people of Allah سبحانه وتعالى, the messengers or prophets, were only guided to a better spiritual state after receiving revelation from Allah سبحانه وتعالى. When we are elevated by Allah سبحانه وتعالى to a noble level, we should always remain humble and remember our pasts and appreciate His guidance to civility with the advent of Islam. Also, it is not befitting that the gifts of Allah become a reason for us to quarrel with one another.

Discussion Question(s)

1. Why is it good to reflect on the bad situations you went through in the past?

56. Baldie

Salem was tired of hearing people call him "Baldie", so he decided to do something about it. Though expensive, he decided to undergo an expensive surgical hair implantation procedure. After a few years, his hair grew long, and he started being addressed by his actual name. Salem enjoyed this change, until he took notice of a change in his social group. In the past, insincere friendship was something he had no reason to deal with. He began to miss the company of the people who used to call him "Baldie".

In practice...

We need not bother about others' opinions, especially if these are related to the externalities. Physical appearance is usually an illusion that prevents us from properly assessing others. It may be wise to train ourselves to care less about others' opinions.

Discussion Question(s)

1. What (if any) is it about your outward appearance that affects how others deal with you?

57. Seeking Guidance

Over the years, Salik had always wondered, "Why do some people receive guidance and know about Allah سبحانه وتعالى, but others don't?" One day, he visited one of his friends who just converted to Islam. His friend was so humble that he even regarded the young children as his teachers. Salik thought to himself, "I think I have found my answer: Humility!"

In practice...

If we undergo a genuine struggle and have the sincere intention of learning, Allah سبحانه وتعالى can inspire an answer to a question, even after many years in our quest for such knowledge. It is not unusual to read stories about the *awliyah*s of Allah سبحانه وتعال, who struggled with a problem and years later, a resolution was inspired by Allah سبحانه وتعالى. In practice, Divine guidance is often associated with humility and self-denial. There may be people with access to the authentic path, but due to their arrogance or other reasons, they fail to engage in the right practice. Similarly, Satan was a very intelligent being, but he was misguided due to his pride and arrogance.

Discussion Question(s)

1. Why is arrogance a trait that is so disdained by Allah سبحانه وتعالى؟

58. No Armor

There was a Muslim lady who used to recite her protection prayers and litanies in the morning and night. One day, she was lazy and was unable to wake up early in the morning to perform this daily routine before leaving home for work. She had a very bad day. At the end of day, she reflected on how she fared during the day and said loudly to herself, "I left my armor at home."

In practice...

It is strongly recommended that we fortify ourselves each day and night with authentic prayers of protection [22]. If we fail to do, we may expect to experience unfavorable situations during the night or the day. We are expected to have total reliance on Allah سبحانه وتعالى through regular prayers of protection from evil and bad outcomes [23] .

Discussion Question(s)

1. Why is it so hard for most people to realize the value and potency of protection prayers (or litanies)?

59. One Hand, One Leg, One Eye

In the past, Dina engaged in a bizarre practice of imitating those with physical disabilities: In secret, she would encase one hand in a cast for a week and use only the other hand throughout the entire week. The next month, she used crutches, moving around with a single leg. Yet, during the upcoming month, she will place an eye patch to cover one of her eyes so she could only see with the aid of a single eye. She was always able to do all these in secret and would usually disguise herself. She believed she was able to evade all scrutiny until a day when her close friend who had been suspicious of her weird actions finally confronted her. Dina said, "I will tell you the reason only because you probably think I am crazy. I desire to appreciate what Allah سبحانه وتعالى has given me. Sometimes, I see people failing to appreciate Allah's سبحانه وتعالى numerous bounties and He tests them with difficulties. I want to truly feel this appreciation for Allah سبحانه وتعالى before such trial or evil befalls me." Her friend was dumbfounded, and Dina concluded, "You may still think that I am crazy, but it doesn't matter."

In practice...

Showing constant gratitude to Allah سبحانه وتعالى for His numerous favors is expected of us. As humans, we often fail to value what we own or possess. Usually, we only value these possessions when we lose them. On the other hand, we are usually envious of what we do not have. In the story, Dina was trying to train train her own ego to truly show appreciation to Allah سبحانه وتعالى.

Discussion Question(s)

1. Why is it so hard to be appreciative of our blessings?

60. Bottom of the Barrel

As was her norm each morning, Nour would make some coffee. Today, she started pouring water from her water jug to fill the coffee maker. As she poured the water, the top of her jug fell off and hit the floor. Nour wondered why this happened. After she finished pouring the water, she peered into the coffee maker's water tank and saw a gooey black substance at the bottom. Then, she smiled to herself, "Clear the dirt from your mind and heart before you fill it with knowledge." She emptied the water, cleaned the tank, and re-filled it.

In practice...

There are meanings and signs in every detail of life. Everything happens with an external and internal reason. If we do not ignore these signs, then we can use each moment of our lives to our advantage. With the acknowledgment of these signs, life's incidents become more purposeful. Positive signs may come from Allah سبحانه وتعالى as long as we have the intention of struggling to regularly maintain our prayers to Allah سبحانه وتعالى [21]. We must also remember that humans can misinterpret the meanings behind these events.

Discussion Question(s)

1. Can you think of a simple event in your life that had a hidden

   (internal) meaning behind it?

61. Remembering Role Models

One day, Hadia woke up feeling uneasy. She remembered the wonderful days she spent in the company of her teacher. Her teacher was a true role model. She was gentle, nice, and patient. She did not take haste in correcting peoples' shortcomings. Her style of communication was filled with wisdom and empathy. Hadia considered the desirable qualities of her teacher and felt ashamed of her own inadequacies. She said to herself, "I am not living up to my potential. However, I will not give up."

In practice...

We should always strive to improve ourselves. Acknowledging our mistake or misdeed is an important step towards spiritual reformation. We should not give up the struggle because it is difficult. Teachers, as role models, are present to show to their students that the struggle can be overcome and that there are other humans who can thrive in this self-struggle. In all stages of life, we should always remain humbly, and seek assistance and guidance from Allah سبحانه وتعالى.

Discussion Question(s)

1. What do you seek in a role model?

62. Weakness and Power

Lately, Farah started feeling old and weak. This really baffled her because she was only 22 years old. She wondered if her condition was related to her diet or sleeping habit. Then, she thought about some Muslims who were at least octogenarians, but were still more active than some youngsters. These group of old people were extensively involved in social work and spent a lot of their time worshiping Allah سبحانه وتعالى. Then, she smiled to herself, "Maybe that is the reason. They have a need and ask the One who can fulfill it."

In practice...

One of the prayers that is recited after each prayer is asking Allah سبحانه وتعالى to help us worship Him in an easy and enjoyable manner [24]. This prayer is one of the famous prayers of Prophet Muhammad ﷺ. As we face different challenges in life with increasing age and deteriorating health, our energies or the zeal for worship and doing good, may not be at the desired level. Therefore, it is very important to ask Allah سبحانه وتعالى to empower us with good actions and worship until our demise.

Discussion Question(s)

1. Compared to older people, why do young people have a harder time asking Allah سبحانه وتعالى for their needs?

63. Disconnecting

One day, a shaykh was teaching his students about the importance of disconnecting from the physical world. The teacher taught *Dhikr*, and how one should focus on Allah سبحانه وتعالى, rather than the noises, lights, temperature, or any other variables in the physical environment. The shaykh explained, "You empty the vessel of its contents. Then you fill it with sweet and wholesome drink."

In practice...

Dhikr requires focus and dedication. One of the famous *adthkar* is *La ilaha illa Allah*. Through this, we try to expunge everything from our heart and focus only on the One and Only Creator, Allah سبحانه وتعالى. By doing so, the sincere worshipper discharges himself (herself) from all worries, stresses, anxieties, and fears [4].

Discussion Question(s)

1. What is it about the human nature that makes it so hard for us to focus on Allah سبحانه وتعالى?

64. Salam!

There was a man who was known to greet everyone very loudly in the local mosque. When this man approached, Abdul Lateef prolonged his *Dhikr* to avoid being disturbed. After a while, everyone in the mosque started exchanging greetings. Abdul Lateef smiled and said to himself, "Even though I don't like his loud voice, I think this man revived a good practice. At least people are following the *Sunnah*."

In practice...

It is virtuous to greet each other with warmth and smiles. The Prophet ﷺ explains that exchanging greetings is one of the rights we have over one another [2]. However, some Muslims, as in the story, prefer silence and solitude. Abdul Lateef avoided socializing with the man, but when he observed that the man's actions encouraged greetings among the congregants, he disagreed with his own initial reaction and secretly applauded the man for reviving something good."

Discussion Question(s)

1. What does it mean to revive a *sunnah*?

65. The Professor

Rumaysah is an Instructor at the local college. She felt disrespected by some of our students during the last semester. She thought to herself, "I need to tough it out." As the semester progressed, Rumaysah gained empathy for these students and became good friends with most of them. At the end of the semester, one of the students adjudged her class as the best he had ever taken. The department chair saw this review, congratulated her, and offered her a promotion. Rumaysah was glad and she said silently to herself, "After every difficulty, there is ease."

In practice...

It is important to exercise patience in all situations and relationships. Husband-wife relationships, student-teacher relations, parent-children relationships, etc. all require patience to be successful. In the story, despite her students' insolence, Rumaysah empathized with them. After this self-struggle, she was rewarded with ease, commendation, and a professional elevation. Allah سبحانه وتعالى promises us in the Quran[vii] : "There is ease after every difficulty." We will get rewarded for our self-struggle both in this world and the afterlife.

Discussion Question(s)

1. What can you do to exercise patience while going through a

   difficulty?

66. Snacks Decreed

One day, a mentally challenged stranger visited the local mosque. He visited during Ramadan but did not realize that everyone was fasting. He had some snacks in his bag and wanted to share them with the congregation. He approached Yunus and offered him a snack. Yunus tried explaining to the stranger that he was fasting. The stranger persisted. Yunus wanted to avoid a confrontation, so he took the snack, kept it aside and continued with his worship. After a while, a traveler came to the mosque looking tired. Yunus thought to himself, "Now, I get the message," and he gave the snack to the traveler. The traveler was pleased and they both smiled.

In practice...

There is meaning in everything. Nothing is random if we can understand it. The travelers, the sick, and mentally ill are all exempt from fasting. In the story, Yunus refrained from arguing with the stranger because it would be a futile exercise. On the other hand, he had no insight into the incidence between himself and the stranger, until a traveler arrived the mosque.

Discussion Question(s)

1. How does this story corroborate the Islamic perspective that our

    Creator already has our sustenance sorted out for us?

67. Mission Accomplished

Nuba used to have a difficult time fasting. Whenever she went without food or drink, she would get tired and suffer headaches. However, breaking the fast was enjoyable for her. With this dilemma of pain and joy, she always had a hard time choosing to fast or not. At the time of breaking the fast, she would forget all the pain that she endured through the day and say *"Alhamdulillah"* from the depths of her heart. She grew confident, happy, and focused after fasting.

In practice...

Fasting is a difficult practice that can help us attain self-restrain and discipline our ego. The ritual entails abstinence from food, drink, and lawful spousal relationships from sunrise to sunset. Compared to the other forms of worship, Allah سبحانه وتعالى rewards the fasting person in a special manner. The Prophet ﷺ says, "The fasting person has two rewards: one at the time of breaking the fast and the other is in the afterlife, where they are amazed with the enormous awards from Allah سبحانه وتعالى [10] [2]." Nuba, in the story experienced the utmost pleasure and happiness at the time of breaking the fast. She felt better after this spiritual achievement. She also expects to be rewarded in the afterlife.

Discussion Question(s)

1. Why is it so much easier to fast during the month of Ramadan than

    during other months?

68. Patience and Prayer

Ilyas easily gets annoyed with his children. He would often yell and scream at them, especially when they disorganize the house. After expressing his anger, he will feel bad and reproach himself, "I wish I was patient and could be nicer to my kids." This was the same scenario each day: A cycle of yells and show of remorse. One day, he thought to himself, "I am making myself miserable with this situation. I need to do something." After a while, he smiled and said, "*Alhamdulillah*, I now know what to do. I need to exercise more patience, but I cannot be patient unless I am strong. And I cannot be strong, until I make my relationship with Allah سبحانه وتعالى stronger. He prayed and asked for help from Allah سبحانه وتعالى.

In practice...

Patience is not just an abstract notion [25]. The trait solidifies in one's character with constant and regular prayers. Hence, the existence of the five daily prayers. Depending on the need and situation, one can increase these daily engagements to be spiritually stronger. In the story, Ilyas needed to exercise more patience in dealing with his children. He realized his shortcoming and constantly blamed himself. It is a praiseworthy effort on the path of Allah سبحانه وتعالى to suppress the ego and blame ourselves instead of blaming others.

Discussion Question(s)

1. Describe some practical ways to train yourself to be more patient

69. Bromance

Muadh came from overseas to visit his friend, Ahmed, in America. Many years had passed since their last encounter. Ahmed waited at the airport to pick up his friend. As soon as Muadh cleared the airport security, he saw Ahmed. The friends were so glad to see each other that they both had tears in their misty eyes. Muadh greeted his old companion and gave him a warm embrace, but his American Muslim friend was not comfortable and said to his friend, "In this country, seeing two men hug one another may lead to unpalatable insinuations." Muadh was surprised and asked his friend to further explain his reservation. Ahmed responded, "I will explain later."

In practice...

In most cultures, casual greetings and salutations involve exchange of hugs and warm embraces. Same-gender hugging or handholding do not necessarily imply a romantic relationship. As practiced in some of the Muslim cultures, these are cultural expressions of brotherhood, love, and geniality. It is not uncommon for men in these societies to shed tears while expressing happiness during a reunion with a friend or family.

Discussion Question(s)

1. Can two individuals of the same gender have a strong non-romantic love for one another?

70. Happy External, Sad Internal

There were two friends with very different personalities: One was always serious and the other was a bit of a joker. One day, the former asked his silly friend, "Why do you always make jokes, even when we are dealing with a serious issue? He continued, "You never cease in your witticism even if we are discussing the afterlife, death, accountability, prayer, etc." In response, his friend pretended to smirk and smiled, "the heart is the home of reflection."

In practice...

Although striving on the path of Allah سبحانه وتعالى is a very important and serious undertaking, we should not lose our sense of humor, albeit without making others feel uncomfortable. Most of the time, the separation between piety and lack thereof can be due to external interactions. All the internal interactions (which is the essence of choosing the path of Allah سبحانه وتعالى) is only undertaken for Allah سبحانه وتعالى and to please Allah سبحانه وتعالى. It is true that the Prophet ﷺ used to say: "If you knew what I knew, then you would laugh less but cry a lot [10] [2]." Yet, *Rasulullah* ﷺ used to sit with his companions, listen to their jokes and smile with them. He is also reported to have used witticism in teaching his companions some wisdom and truth. The Prophet ﷺ never made the people around him uncomfortable. The Quran praises this quality of

Rasulullah ﷺ and mentions that if the Prophet ﷺ was harsh, then the people

would not have loved to be around him[viii].

Discussion Question(s)

1. How can one balance between light heartedness and seriousness?

71. The Full Story

Recently, a man started passing the night in the local mosque. The regular congregants were not familiar with him and felt uncomfortable with this perceived stranger. One day, alone in the mosque with the man, Adam approached him and enquired about his situation. The man explained that his mother recently passed away, and that he was trying to reconnect with Allah سبحانه وتعالى after being distant from his religion for a long time. Adam chided himself for his hitherto unsavory opinion of the man. The next day, as usual, the man was observed sleeping in the mosque and one of mosque's administrators reprimanded him harshly, "This is a mosque and you cannot make this place your bed!" Adam witnessed this encounter and felt bad about it. At the end of the prayer, he courageously made an announcement in the mosque. He introduced the stranger to everyone and clarified that he did not pose a danger to anyone.

In practice...

It is very important to empathize with everyone. Adam understood the man's situation after having a discussion with him. It is common for us to need more help, camaraderie, and support when we experience a loss. As such, it is not uncommon to observe that some people sleep and spend more time in the mosques during such periods in their lives. Adam handled the case with wisdom by not directly confronting the harsh administrator but rather by introducing the man to the entire congregation. This is similar to how *Rasulullah* ﷺ solved some issues among his companions. The Prophet ﷺ never targeted any specific individual to reprimand him (her). Rather, he passed across the intended teaching(s) by introducing general guidelines to everyone [20].

Discussion Question(s)

1. How can we have the best opinions of others without being taken advantage of?

72. Gradual Increase

Amal loved coffee a lot. However, yesterday, she started her day by only drinking warm water instead of coffee. Then as time passes throughout the day, she increased its strength by increasingly adding small amounts of coffee. She really desired the caffeine rush all at once, but new small steady steps were necessary to achieve the desired effect.

In practice...

Training and learning come in stages. The path of Allah سبحانه وتعالى requires constant self-struggle and spiritual advancements come with small increments. It is important to avoid trying to accomplish several commendable actions all at once.

Discussion Question(s)

1. Can you think of some examples of how you could build your spiritual habits in small progressive increments?

73. Verily, Allah is with the Patient

There was a young lady who found it difficult to control her temper. She would usually suffer the consequence after each episode. Each time she lost her temper, she would regret her action and blame herself for not being patient enough. In an attempt to change her tendency, she started reading the Holy Quran and reviewed all the verses on patience. Then, she felt better and promised herself to be more mindful of her words and actions so she could imbibe this lofty virtue.

In practice...

Patience is an important spiritual virtue. It is a continuous struggle to embody the true meaning of patience. One way of adopting the virtue is through prayer. Another way is to be constantly mindful that any seemingly evil occurrences can turn out good if one is patient. Patience is enjoined on us in different verses of the Holy Quran. Allah سبحانه وتعالى is the supporter of the patient one and we should always rely on Him alone. We should exercise patience when faced with evil, we should be patient in our struggle in the path of Allah سبحانه وتعالى, we should be patient at all times. If we resort to complaints or continue to blame others for any misfortune that befalls us, then we have failed to exercise patience [2]. If we fall into this entrapment, our relationship with Allah سبحانه وتعالى becomes unstable and unfruitful. Rather, we should engage in the Muslim practice of *Dhikr* of

Alhamdullilah to appreciate Allah سبحانه وتعالى, and under circumstances where utmost patience is required, we should recite, *hasbiyallah*, {Allah سبحانه وتعالى is sufficient for me}.

Discussion Question(s)

1. Describe how Prayer is related to patience

74. No Pain, No Gain

Yasmin knew about the benefits of fasting, but the pain of hunger frightened her. As such, she was always hesitant to observe any optional fasting. However, after fasting, she would feel much stronger. She also realized that when she neglected fasting for too long, she became weaker.

In practice...

Fasting is a pillar of Islam that focuses on the mind and heart. It helps to eliminate stress and anxiety. Apart from the mandatory fasting during the Islamic holy month of Ramadan, the Prophetic recommendations for voluntary fasting include fasting on the three middle days in the Islamic lunar months, and fasting on Mondays and Thursdays[2]. In the story, although it was difficult for her, Yasmin benefited from fasting.

Discussion Question(s)

1. What is the wisdom in having so much benefit with difficult tasks?

75. The Focused Muslim

One day, Abdul Qadir, was in the mosque. Two people started arguing about a religious issue. Abdul Qadir thought to himself "I won't get involved," and tried to focus on his supplications. Finally, those involved in the argument left. And Abdul Qadir slowly exhaled, "*Alhamdulillah*, {thanks to Allah سبحانه وتعالى.}" A few minutes later, more people started arguing. Abdul Qadir now thought to himself, "Maybe, this is a sign. Let me move to my car in the parking lot to complete my prayer and meditation." He did as he planned and later returned to the mosque. On his return, he found the mosque peaceful and calm. Then, he serenely completed his meditation and concluded with "*Alhamdulillah*, {thanks to Allah سبحانه وتعالى}."

In practice...

Full focus is required during prayers and meditations. Prayers and meditations help us strengthen ourselves spiritually. If we find ourselves in situations that affect our concentration and focus, it is incumbent on us to seek an alternate location for our prayers and meditations. Mosques are places to find tranquility, calmness, and peace for our prayers. However, if there is the possibility of disturbance or evil outcomes, we may leave the mosque until the negativity is gone.

Discussion Question(s)

1. Why do we often disrespect the sanctity of our mosques?

76. A Pseudo Altercation in the Mosque

Last week, there were two congregants arguing in the mosque. One was an Arab and the other was an Indian. The Arab said, "You are neglecting the *sunnah muakkadah*." The Indian replied, "I only follow the Prophet ﷺ." Asif looked at both men, smiled, and silently chuckled, "The main point was lost in translation".

In practice...

We should acknowledge others' cultural, ethnic, and gender backgrounds. In the story, the two men who practice the same faith, thought they differed on a religious matter. They used different words to describe the same practice. The term *sunnah muakkadah* refers to Prophetic practice. There was no contradiction in their positions.

Discussion Question(s)

1. Are there more misunderstandings in religious matters than worldly matters? Why?

77. The Muslim, the semi-Muslim Buddhist and their Teachers

There once lived a Muslim and a Buddhist. They were bosom friends. Surprisingly, the Buddhist also had teachers from the Muslim tradition. They would continuously argue about whose teachers were better. It seems that they both somewhat missed the salient point of embarking on a spiritual path.

In practice...

A wise Muslim tries to avoid religious arguments, especially about the superiority of one's religion or teachers over others. Nowadays, it is quite common to find people simultaneously following half of the teachings of one path and adhering to the teachings of another spiritual path. Unfortunately, the arguments about the superiority of teachers or schools of thoughts is nothing new. Genuine Muslims are not trapped in these futile arguments. Rather, they follow what they are comfortable with and allow others to seek the truth as they seem fit.

Discussion Question(s)

1. Why are people hesitant to fully commit to a specific religious tradition or school of thought?

78. Recite Now, Reward Later

Taha sat alone in the mosque, enjoying reading the Noble Quran, praying, and reflecting on the Quranic verses. Later, a group of people entered the mosque with the body of a deceased Muslim for funeral preparations. Taha still tried to continue his recitations but was distracted by the tears of the deceased's family members bemoaning their loss. Afterwards, the family members left the prayer area, leaving only Taha in the mosque. He completed his recitations, smiled and admonished himself, "This is life. You recite while alive. You have some interaction with people, but at the end, the people all leave and once again, you are alone with your Quran."

In practice...

Death is a reality. It is not an ominous transition if it is internalized through practice and worship before it occurs. In the story, Taha understood that having a real connection with the Holy Quran will help our situation after our transition.

Discussion Question(s)

1. Does reciting the Quran remind you of death? Does seeing the remains of the deceased remind you of the Quran?

79. The Forbearing Muslim

One Friday afternoon, Hashim was in the mosque praying and reading the Noble Quran. There were also two talkative youths in the mosque. Others in the mosque treated them poorly, but Hashim treated them gently and kindly. They knew and liked Hashim, and wished to consult him, but they also knew that they should not disturb him during his prayers. While waiting, the two youths observed an old man walk up to Hashim and sat next to him. In general, Hashim would not permit any distraction while reading the Quran, but on that day, he paused his recitations and attended to the old man. After his consultation with Hashim, the old man happily left the mosque. The two youths were encouraged by Hashim's response and they also approached him. Like before, Hashim responded kindly and warmly received them. Afterwards, Hashim remarked, "Today is a special day, Friday. I should be forbearing."

In practice...

If a person is enjoying a nice sweet dessert, he (she) may not wish to be disturbed [27]. For some Muslim scholars, one's relationship with Allah سبحانه وتعالى in the prayers and reading the Quran can have a similar sweet taste. In the story, Hashim had such an experience with his prayers and recitations of the Quran. However, he understood the desire of the three men to have discussions with him and he patiently obliged them.

Discussion Question(s)

1. How can we convince ourselves to willingly deal with other

   people's concerns and apprehensions?

80. Sunset Reflections

One Sunday evening, Sharifa sat in the mosque, appreciating the approaching sunset and the natural breeze coming through the mosque's open windows. She looked back upon some old memories, especially when she was less spiritually inclined. She felt she had wasted a huge part of her life and she remarked to herself "I wish I knew then, what I now know."

In practice...

One of the ways to ascertain improvement on the path of Allah سبحانه وتعالى is that we do not desire a return to our previous state. However, it is normal to miss old friends, places, and good experiences [28]. We should constantly learn and increase our knowledge in the relationship with Allah سبحانه وتعالى. Each day should be better (in such relationship with Allah سبحانه وتعالى) than the previous one.

Discussion Question(s)

1. How do we strike a balance between excessive regret and beneficial remorse?

81. Decisions, Decisions

Ali and his wife, Ruquyya, were trying to decide which teacher to choose for their children's religious education. The wife said, "Let us decide and get it over with," and her husband replied, "I am not sure which one is better." They discussed the issue without reaching a conclusion, until they both became tired. After a few hours, Ruquyya received a text from one of the potential teachers saying, "I have fallen gravely ill; it is no longer feasible for me to teach your child." In response, Ali exclaimed, "*Alhamdulillah*, the decision is made."

In practice...

In making choices, people often use logic and their minds to make life decisions. Islam advocates positive and active submission and surrender to Allah سبحانه وتعالى. One may call this reliance or *tawakkul*. It is positive because we do not see this relationship as a passive submission to an authority. The One Who is Caring, Merciful and at the same time the Most Powerful and Wise, can do anything for us if we submit and surrender to His will. This approach takes away all the burden of worries, stress, and unnecessary apprehensions from our spiritual shoulders. As in the story, submission or reliance can be explicit. In other cases, it may be implicit, so we should understand the *adab* of the path.

Discussion Question(s)

1. What stops people from being decisive?

82. Blessed Coffee

There was once a class with a religious scholar who was also famous for making coffee. The religious scholar would often make coffee for the students before class. Zaid asked if the scholar could teach him how to make coffee. The scholar replied, "OK, first you say "*Bismillah* {In the name of Allah سبحانه وتعالى}, then put the filter in place and pour the water with your right hand. It is important to use a natural filter and make the coffee light. Place seven small spoons of coffee beans in the filter while saying *Bismillah*. Enjoy its aroma while it brews and serve it as soon as it is done so that it does not get bitter. This is the recipe of my famous coffee."

In practice...

It is important to invoke the Creator's name in our foods and drinks to receive blessings from Allah سبحانه وتعالى. The *Dhikr* is the recognition of the blessings of Allah سبحانه وتعالى [29]. According to some Muslims, foods and drinks taste better with the mention of Allah سبحانه وتعالى. It is the practice of the Prophet ﷺ to favor the use of odd numbers (such as 7 in the story). The scholar was careful to choose an organic coffee filter. He also advocated the use of natural and organic ingredients,[7] as suggested by the Quran.

Discussion Question(s)

1. What does it mean for food to have blessings in it?

---

[7] tayyib

83. A Mother's Mercy

Idris's wife complained to him about all the bad things their children did on a fateful day. She said the children no longer listen to her and that she felt helpless as a mother. Idris said to himself, "If I discipline them, I may be too harsh. I won't do anything and just watch what happens." Days passed, and the mother became uneasy about the children's insolent behavior, and the fact that she was further losing control of the situation. Finally, Idris said to himself, "I think I need to do something drastic." He called his two children and enumerated all the blames that were reported by their mother. The children were silent, and he declared, "One of you needs to sleep upstairs and the other downstairs. You will not sleep in your beds tonight because of what has been happening lately." Both children burst out weeping. The mother was troubled, and her heart broken. She tried to persuade Idris to review the punishment, but he remained firm, thinking, "*SubhanAllah.* If this is the mercy of the mother, what about the mercy of Allah? سبحانه وتعالى."

In practice...

It is important to realize that there is an accountability in this world and afterlife. We have varying degrees of ethical or moral standards. Some may avoid evil due to its worldly consequences. Others may not engage in evil because it will affect their spiritual state. The most desirous approach in the path of Allah سبحانه وتعالى is to perform good actions and avoid evils to please Allah سبحانه وتعالى. We should aim for this lofty intention when we consider that Allah سبحانه وتعالى is willing to forgive us, regardless of our shortcomings. Considering how merciful the mother was with her children, it is a shame that they would push the boundaries until they deserved punishment.

Discussion Question(s)

1. Can you think of some examples of Allah's mercies, even when we are tested?

84. Protective Jealousy

Isa attended an interfaith meeting. Christians and Muslims were present, and they were discussing about Allah سبحانه وتعالى. Many statements were made. A Christian minister said, "We believe that God is jealous," and a Muslim chaplain replied, "Allah سبحانه وتعالى does not want anyone to be worshiped except Him." They continued their discussions and deliberations. Isa said to himself, "Our beliefs have more in common than we think."

In practice...

It is very important to worship only Allah سبحانه وتعالى. We should keep the proper *adab* and maintain respectful attitude towards Allah سبحانه وتعالى. Jealousy is understood to be positive when one is referencing Allah سبحانه وتعالى, but it can also be alienating due to the popular contemporary use of the word in negative contexts [8].

Discussion Question(s)

1. What are the similarities and differences between Muslims' and Christians' perception of the Creator?

85. The Overflowing Cup

One Sunday evening, Saleh poured coffee into a small cup, trying to dispense as much beverage as possible, until it overflowed. The hot coffee spilled on him, scalding his hands in the process. He said to himself, "I was greedy. I wanted to get more than I could handle. In the end, I got burned."

In practice...

Allah سبحانه وتعالى only gives us what we can handle or what we can bear: tests, tribulations, trials, and spiritual achievements. When we strive to achieve more, it could be difficult and can become an insurmountable challenge. Thus, we should always appreciate Allah سبحانه وتعالى.

Discussion Question(s)

1. Are humans usually aware of their limits or not?

86. Easier Said than Done

Khalil was of a calm disposition and often advised his companions to be the same. He explained to them that everything was decreed by Allah سبحانه وتعالى and that they should not allow hardships overwhelm them. Khalil's life was free of difficulties and he attributed this to his ability to comport himself. On a Saturday afternoon, Khalil was tested with a great trial. He received a call from his parents informing him that his grandfather had suffered a heart attack. Khalil began to weep uncontrollably. His perception of himself and his friends immediately began to change. He now wept for his own hardship and for the hardships of others.

In practice...

It is not always easy to implement all the Islamic teachings that we learn. When a person loses his beloved ones, livelihood, home, or other things he/she is attached to, it is difficult to exercise patience. The trials and tests disconnect the individual from his (her) attachments. Recitation of "*La ilaha illa Allah*" removes the worldly attachments from a person's heart and mind [4].

Discussion Question(s)

1. Why are we sometimes insensitive to the hardship(s) of others?

87. Cruel World

While watching the news, Muminah witnessed a cruel act and she was really traumatized. The pain of the evil remained with her for days. She constantly asked herself, "Why? Why? Why…?" At the same, she asked Allah سبحانه وتعالى to make it easy for her to forget what she saw. After a few days, it was time to move on.

In practice...

Sometimes, endless reasoning and self-conversations can drown a person in pessimism. It is important to ask Allah سبحانه وتعالى to ease our pains during times of evil and continue with our daily routine.

Discussion Question(s)

1. Why is it dangerous to question the decree of Allah سبحانه وتعالى؟

88. Expect the Unexpected

Tahira was happy with her spiritual growth. Every day was filled with contemplating the signs of Allah سبحانه وتعالى, reciting the Noble Quran and pondering her existence. Apart from having too much homework in her Math class, things were quite rosy. However, things became a bit more complicated when her parents finally decided to divorce. She felt a deep pain in their decision. Fortunately, her spiritual regiment had prepared her for the anguish. She knew that every difficulty is succeeded by something good, and she always console herself thus: "I plan and Allah سبحانه وتعالى plans. I just need to submit and ask for the good outcome of this change from Allah سبحانه وتعالى". She also realized that she was getting older and she will remember death by reminding herself, "*Alhamdullillah*, I will meet with Allah سبحانه وتعالى soon. I hope all the changes will ultimately benefit me *inshAllah*."

In practice...

As believers, we should always prepare for the unexpected. Initially, it can be painful, but ultimately, we can mitigate our pains with prayers and recitations from the Noble Quran (understanding and personalizing them to suit our situation). In these unknowns, one should always try the easy and natural way: submission to Allah سبحانه وتعالى and trust in Him alone.

On the other hand, incessant complaints will only cause us to lose energy

unnecessarily. Another effective way of coping with any type of grief is

embracing the reality of death. When we acknowledge that this life is

ephemeral and that we will eventually meet with the Lover—Allah سبحانه

وتعالى—, then we would get relief from our griefs.

Discussion Question(s)

1. What are some of the other ways we can prepare ourselves for

   hardship?

89. Ups and Downs

Rabia has difficulty understanding the meanings in peoples' lives. She realized that sometimes, evil befalls people and they become sad. Sometimes, they are happy. Yet, sometimes, they are somewhere in the middle. Everything comes full circle.

In practice...

We should understand that Allah سبحانه وتعالى changes the conditions of people throughout their lives. The Holy Quran uses an expression that can be roughly translated as "rotating the days among people." From this expression, a possible wisdom in the change of peoples' condition is to evaluate if they will maintain their appreciation to Allah سبحانه وتعالى in good, evil, and neutral times. Hence, one of the goals on the path of Allah سبحانه وتعالى should be the continuous growth of one's gratitude to Allah سبحانه وتعالى in all conditions: adversity, joy, and neutrality [30].

Discussion Question(s)

1. How do we remain stable while going through the vicissitudes of life?

90. Spiritual Discoveries

Afiyah would usually get ill on Mondays when she was not fasting. She would often receive bad news on Thursdays when she did not fast. Then, she deduced that Monday fasting prevents sicknesses and Thursday fasting shields against evils. Few weeks ago, she fasted on a Monday but still got ill. Then, she said to herself: "Either my intuition has an exception to it, or it is simply wrong."

In practice...

Religious laws impose boundaries or limits with logic. If we fail to follow a religious guideline or law, then we will be held responsible by Allah سبحانه وتعالى [30]. Conversely, personal spiritual discoveries can either be right or wrong. They have no religious requirements, but if a person follows these discoveries, he(she) may receive gifts in this world and afterlife. Although there is wisdom in adhering to religious laws or guidelines, a believer does it or performs it because Allah سبحانه وتعالى directed it. This wisdom may or may not be known to us. The intent is not to implement the Creator's injunctions for their benefits, but to please Allah سبحانه وتعالى.

Discussion Question(s)

1. Why is it important for us to make sure the rules of the religion govern our spirituality?

91. The River of Life

Malak was lost in thoughts, pondering on the recent events in her life. She was pushed by the tides of life towards directions she least expected. Nothing was going as she planned. She asked herself, "What are the wisdoms behind these trials from Allah سبحانه وتعالى؟"

In practice...

Unexpected things may happen in one's life. These events may look good, evil, or neutral. It is important to deduce meanings from these personal or social events. In the story, Malak was trying to understand if her challenges were tests from Allah سبحانه وتعالى. The purpose of a test or trial is to either elevate our spiritual state or to reveal our real character: evil or good.

Discussion Question(s)

1. Is it always wise for us to assess the reason(s) behind the events in our life? Why or Why not?

92. The Hailstorm

There once lived a Muslim lady who had a very special relationship with Allah سبحانه وتعالى. One day, she got afflicted with something evil and planned to address the issue: Foremost, she prayed to Allah سبحانه وتعالى. Then, she tried to understand the affliction. She said to herself, "I need the opinion of at least three people who really love me and are willing to help me deal with this evil." She approached a close neighbor for her opinion, but as soon as she tried to broach the issue, a hail shower began outside. The Muslim lady paused, restrained herself from discussing the issue with her friend and contemplated the meaning of the sudden hail shower. Then, she visited another friend to discuss the problem. Again, as soon as she tried discussing the issue, another hail shower started, and this friend had to excuse herself to pick up her kids from school. The Muslim lady reflected on her approach to the problem and felt pained that she desired to share her problem with others rather than with Allah سبحانه وتعالى. She intensified her prayers and smiled, "Surely, Allah سبحانه وتعالى does not want me to share my problems with anyone else. Allah سبحانه وتعالى is sufficient for me! What a Friend! What a Supporter!"

In practice...

Some mystics and Islamic scholars contend that discussing one's problems with others is disrespectful to Allah سبحانه وتعالى. In the story, the protagonist interpreted the hail showers as signs that her existing close relationship with Allah سبحانه وتعالى suffices for her needs. Prophet Muhammad ﷺ thought his companions this supplication: "*Hasbiya Allah La ilaha illa Hu Alayhi Tawwakaltu wa Huwa Rabbul Arshil Azim*, {Allah سبحانه وتعالى is Sufficient for me, there is no deity except Allah سبحانه وتعالى, I rely on Allah سبحانه وتعالى and Allah سبحانه وتعالى is the Most Exalted High Holder of Authority and Dominance}" [24].

Discussion Question(s)

1. How does one practically rely on Allah سبحانه وتعالى؟

93. The Daily Deception

When Maha wakes up in the morning, she usually feels energetic, powerful, and hopeful. In contrast, when she goes to bed, she feels tired and weak. One weekend, a powerful thought crossed her mind: What is real? What is deception? Am I strong? Am I weak? At that moment, she received a text about a funeral prayer in the mosque. She chided herself: "Now I understand. Strong or weak, Death is the reality."

In practice...

Life is transient and the reality of death corroborates this fact. A known spiritual disease is the deception of living while being oblivious of death. The reality of death serves as a balance in our worldly existence. Some Muslim scholars think that most of the pains associated with losing material things in life is due to this disease of not contemplating death[8].

Discussion Question(s)

1. Why aren't we strong all the time? Why are we tested with weakness?

---

[8]   This disease is called "*tulu-amal*" in Sufi terminology.

94. Boundaries

Lut once attended an interfaith gathering, where there was a discussion on the piety of the righteous sages and their importance as role models for humanity. One of the Muslim attendees cited the life of a scholar from his own tradition as an example of these righteous sages. Lut made a joke about the story, and everyone burst into laughter. Horrified, Lut paused for a minute and he silently sighed, "What have I done?

In practice...

We should respect Islamic beliefs, values, elders, and scholars. Although we live in liberal societies where witticism is tolerated, the *awliya* of Allah ﷺ believe that jokes should have limits and should not be about sacred items. The state of being with Allah سبحانه وتعالى and friendship with Allah سبحانه وتعالى requires proper respect and *adab*. Often, people lose their good friends due to inappropriate speech. Having respectful boundaries with the sacred—Allah سبحانه وتعالى, the Quran, the Prophet ﷺ, the Hadith, and the genuine scholars —is important for progress on the path of Allah سبحانه وتعالى.

Discussion Question(s)

1. What are the benefits and potential harms of jokes?

95. Learning to Wait

Kareema was teaching a lesson on the prophetic character to some elementary school students. The students tried to ask her questions, but she deliberately ignored them. She just smiled and continued reading from the assigned book. After a while, the students took a cue from her and started following her readings. Little did they know that the *adab* they were learning from their teacher was a greater lesson than the answer to any of their questions.

In practice...

Asking a question at an inappropriate time or place may make us deduce wrong meanings. This can alienate an earnest learner from genuine learning. A proven genuine way of learning is to be with a teacher and learn (and observe) natural discourses, occurring events, and then deduce the meanings. Of course, formal answers to peoples' questions and enquiries also foster the learning process. However, the questions must be asked at the appropriate place and time.

Discussion Question(s)

1. Why is it important for instructors to teach their students good behaviors and manners?

96. The Reality of Longing

Fatima would often think about her past. She would feel pains in longing for her old friends, deceased parents, siblings, and cherished places. One day, she again remembered all these nice memories. However, she felts no pains. She thought and said to herself: "Everything that I miss is temporary. I accord them value as if they are permanent and can benefit me. I think I just miss Allah سبحانه وتعالى, who is my Friend, regardless of time and place."

In practice...

It is normal to be saddened by memories, especially of good teachers, parents, and friends. But all created beings have limits and your love for them should have limits as well. According them too much value can be painful. Compared to all other missed items, Allah سبحانه وتعالى knows and appreciates our longing for Him [31]. These emotions, feelings, and thoughts towards Allah سبحانه وتعالى can elevate our status with Him.

Discussion Question(s)

1. How does one overcome the pain of loss?

97. The Difficulty of Being Human

Anisa usually contemplated the difficulty of being a human. One day, she reminded herself: "I should not break anyone's heart. I should be nice. I should be fair. I should not be angry. I should not be jealous. I should truly appreciate Allah سبحانه وتعالى." As she thought of more things to do and those to avoid, she silently lamented, "Indeed, the inheritance of Adam is weighty. *Alhamdulillah*, at least, I am trying."

In practice...

It is difficult to be a virtuous human. Anisa's reminders are some of the expected traits or attitudes of a person on the path of spiritual reformation. The most difficult part is not truly appreciating Allah سبحانه وتعالى. But, in the end, Allah سبحانه وتعالى appreciates all our sincere efforts but not the results. Hence, Anisa is grateful to Allah سبحانه وتعالى for being able to try.

Discussion Question(s)

1. What else is hard about being human?

98. Fear and Protection

Sumayah was always afraid: Afraid of people, the unknown, death etc. Today, she recited her protective *duas* but still felt fearful. She said to herself, "I rely on Allah سبحانه وتعالى to bestow on me the benefits of these *duas* in my life."

In practice...

Life is a struggle. We are expected to seek refuge only in Allah سبحانه وتعالى under all circumstances, especially during fearful situations. One may be fearful of others, but we can eradicate this fear by practice, prayer, and self-struggle. Although Sumayah was invoking the Divine phrases and making *Dhikr*, she still felt some fear in her daily discourses and encounters. She concludes that she needs to confront her fears by sole reliance on Allah سبحانه وتعالى.

Discussion Question(s)

1. What stops us from feeling the effect of our worship?

99. See the Beauty

On a cold winter day, Tariq was alone in the mosque reading the Noble Quran. A small fly buzzing around his head was the only visible living being in site. Tariq thought, "*SubhanAllah*! It is amazing to see a fly on a cold winter day. Everything else outside is either dead or inactive because of the snow. How beautiful is life! *Ya-Hayy*!"

In practice...

Anything with life should remind us of Allah سبحانه وتعالى. One of the names of Allah سبحانه وتعالى is *Al-Hayy*, the Source and the Creator of Life. Some invoke this attribute of the Creator in times of depression (and anxiety) to relax and gain strength from Allah سبحانه وتعالى. Several inspirational Muslim stories emphasize respect for (and friendship with) animals. It is not uncommon to read about stories of imprisoned *Awliya* of Allah سبحانه وتعالى, who were known to be friends with animals that are repulsive to most humans (such as flies, snakes, mice, etc.) The *Awliya* of Allah سبحانه وتعالى consider these animals as holders of life, reminding them of their Creator, *Al-Hayy*. They are signs from Allah سبحانه وتعالى if we can understand their meaning and purpose.

Discussion Question(s)

1. What is the relationship between humans and other created living beings?

100. Reliance on Allah سبحانه وتعالى

Ahlam had a very close relationship with Allah سبحانه وتعالى. The Creator honored her with the gift of "answered supplications". Whatever she asked from Allah سبحانه وتعالى, Allah سبحانه وتعالى granted her. One day, she lost her job but hesitated to pray about it. She thought, "I will have *tawakkul* (total reliance on Allah سبحانه وتعالى) and will be content with whatever Allah سبحانه وتعالى chooses for me. I am happy as long as Allah سبحانه وتعالى is pleased with me."

In practice...

Attaining *tawakkul* (total reliance on Allah سبحانه وتعالى) is an important goal on the path towards spiritual reformation. In the story, Ahlam cultivated a very close relationship with Allah سبحانه وتعالى through constant prayers and sincere appreciations. As such, Allah سبحانه وتعالى would always grant her wishes. She attained *tawakkul* and believed that irrespective of any outcome or situation, the pleasure of Allah سبحانه وتعالى is of most paramount importance.

Discussion Question(s)

1. What are some obstacles to our *tawakkul*?

101. Good Opinions II

There was a teenager being mentored by Rayyan. However, the young man rarely showed up on time, if at all. Rayyan consistently counseled him on the importance of trust and time management. He explained to him that he had been offered many opportunities and blessings, and that it was essential to make judicious use of them. All the while, Rayyan's mind was occupied with two things: "1) How to help the young man overcome his faults. 2) How to make excuses for his faults."

In practice...

Allah's سبحانه وتعالى knowledge encompasses all things. As humans, we should try to assist others with our best intentions. In the story, Rayyan did not want to think badly of the young man. It is encouraged that we make good excuses for others and refrain from blaming them for their faults. This is known as *husnu zann*, thinking good about others. The opposite of this is known as *su-i zann*, thinking and assuming bad about others. We are always encouraged to practice *husnu zann* when dealing with our loved ones and humanity at large.

Discussion Question(s)

1. When someone confides in you, how do you avoid judging them?

102. Mind Over Heart

One Saturday morning, Imran had a dispute with his wife. He was unable to control himself and used some harsh language. As he sat in their living room after the altercation, he regretted the cruel treatment of his beloved spouse. He wished he had controlled his emotions, instead of allowing them to control him. He thought to himself, "Indeed, self-restraint is true freedom."

In practice...

It is important to favor our minds over our emotions. Our emotions are not always in harmony with our conscience. The true emotions or inspirations from your conscience do not conflict with the mind, logic, and reason. If they are in conflict, then these emotions can be ego-driven or encouraged by Satan and can lead to evil. At times of conflict or disputes, such inappropriate emotions or thoughts can overpower a person's mind, heart, and conscience.

Discussion Question(s)

1. Is it ever appropriate to follow your emotions and ignore your mind?

103. Moving On

Haniya and her husband had an argument about caring for their newborn. Her husband felt that he was always being forced to carry and babysit the child. A few days after the dispute, her husband was still upset. Haniya had decided not to take the issue personally and could now be seen holding the infant more often. Unfortunately, despite being relieved of his burden, her husband persisted in his grudge. Haniya kept her cool and prayed within herself that he would just "move on".

In practice...

As humans, we are bound to be involved in conflicts or misunderstandings. However, we should endeavor to avoid keeping any grudge after the conflicts, especially when the issue is a misunderstanding between spouses. There are many stories about rulers in Islamic history, whose spouses used to freely criticize and yell at them. These rulers wisely exercised silence and patience, especially in family relations.

Discussion Question(s)

1. Why is it so hard for us to let things go?

104. The Cancer of Arrogance

Waleed's need to rationalize everything made it very difficult for him to connect to his religion. His friend, Musaab, would try to explain to him the importance of submission to Allah سبحانه وتعالى and how it did not conflict with logic. Unfortunately, Musaab was never able to convince him, until Waleed got ill. Waleed was ill for several weeks and was eventually diagnosed with a malignant type of cancer. Musaab was deeply troubled by his friend's sufferings and constantly visited him. He found that the illness had greatly humbled his friend and he was now seriously considering the role of religion in his life. Musaab realizes that although Allah سبحانه وتعالى was testing his friend with an illness, He cured him of a worse disease.

In practice...

Belief inherently demands submission to the Creator. Humility can aid belief and elevate a person before Allah سبحانه وتعالى. Sometimes, hardships can make us livid and even alienate us from Allah سبحانه وتعالى due to frustration and anger. However, we should use hardships to remind us of our weaknesses, needs, and fragility. In this case, hardship is a blessing as it connects us to Allah سبحانه وتعالى.

Discussion Question(s)

1. Arrogance is a grave sin. Can you think of some of its negative

    consequences?

105. Cover your Iman

Haafiz's mom had just placed food on the kitchen table while he spoke on the phone with his friend. As he walked towards the kitchen table, he covered the food and continued with his phone call, speaking about his personal problems and challenges. His mother shook her head and admonished him: "You would be better off protecting your *iman* (belief) than protecting the food".

In practice...

We should be cautious of our relationships and keep the company of people with genuine knowledge. The company of these people should benefit us: we should observe them and ask them questions. With their presence as companions in our lives, they can easily correct us when we err. On the other, bad company can serve as a threat to our *iman*. Associating with them can make us comfortable with backbiting, slandering and other bad habits.

Discussion Question(s)

1. Why do we place more importance on our material wealth than our spiritual wealth?

106. Time Well Spent

On a weekday afternoon, Dhakirah attended a meeting at her work. She was less interested in the meeting proceedings, but she paid attention to avoid being disrespectful. Unfortunately for her, the meeting was extended for another hour. So, she stilled her mind and brought her heart into the remembrance of her Creator. Suddenly, the meeting did not seem to be taking so long.

In practice...

It is important to recognize peoples' spiritual needs. Just as one may need to temporarily leave a meeting for a restroom break, spiritual urges may come at any time and we will need to fulfil these needs too. The five daily prayers throughout the day can serve as an avenue to fulfil these spiritual urges. However, the spiritual urges may still be felt at other times outside the ordained prayer times. As in the story, we do not necessarily need to leave a room, enclosure, or any physical space to fulfil our spiritual needs. Rather, we can transform any undesirable physical state or condition to a virtual space of peace and tranquility by reorienting our minds through a few seconds of remembrance of Allah سبحانه وتعالى (*"Dhikr"*).

Discussion Question(s)

1. What other ways can you incorporate spirituality into your daily

    routine?

107. Peace and Blessings

Sakinah was often anxious. To calm her anxiety, she would usually pace back and forth, but to no avail. She had no solution in sight until she attended a gathering of *salawat* at her local mosque. Now when she needs to feel peace, she simply sends peace on the Prophet ﷺ.

In practice...

When one feels stressed or anxious, it is very critical to remember the one who taught us the solutions to all problems: *Rasulullah* ﷺ. There are several practices of *Dhikr* to remember the Prophet ﷺ in different forms known as *salawat* and *tahiyyat*. In some Muslim cultures, the tradition is to get together and recite these phrases collectively. It is also customary to recite the *dhikrs* daily in times of difficulty and sickness. *Dhikrs* can bring blessings and ease in one's life.

Discussion Question(s)

1. How can reflecting on the life of the Prophet ﷺ impact us in a positive way?

108. The Barber, the Beard and the Accident

Raafi was very proud of his luxuriant and long beard. He would admire himself in the mirror, proud that he was following the ways of the prophets. One day, he went to the barber to trim some extra hair on his neck region. This barber was a Muslim and was often engaged in *Dhikr* and the remembrance of Allah سبحانه وتعالى. While trimming Raafi's hairs, the barber started his *Dhikr*, closed his eyes in a mild trance, and inadvertently shaved off a part of Raafi's beard. Raafi screamed and yelled, "You idiot, don't you respect your beard? It's *Sunnah!*" Shocked, the barber profusely apologized, and responded: "Is bad character, *Sunnah?*"

In practice...

It is *Sunnah*, encouraged, and rewarding to follow the ways of righteous role models such as the prophets and *Awliyaullah*. However, one should remember that doing so may lead to arrogance or an unhealthy attachment. In the story, although Raafi was proud of his beard, any attachment to it can be a test on the path of Allah سبحانه وتعالى if it is not seen as a means to please Him. In other words, the only attachment one should have is to Allah سبحانه وتعالى.

Discussion Question(s)

1. Why do we tend to embrace some Islamic teachings and neglect

   others?

109. Test of Life

Iman had somewhat of a challenge homeschooling her children. Initially, the kids whined about their schoolwork. As they continued studying, they got excited about learning and discovering. Rather than responding to the kids' questions at the beginning of the lessons, she encouraged them to discover the answers themselves. As the lessons progressed, she was amazed about their adaptations and self-satisfactions due to learning by struggle. Iman thought to herself, "If I provided the answers from the beginning, they would not learn this well, and would not enjoy and appreciate the knowledge. *SubhanAllah*, this is similar to the test of life."

In practice...

Allah's سبحانه وتعالى knowledge encompasses everything: past, present, and future. One of the secrets of life is that Allah سبحانه وتعالى creates humans to self-witness their own journey in their relationship with Allah سبحانه وتعالى, just as children go through a learning process. Thus, humans cannot claim otherwise before Allah سبحانه وتعالى on the day of reckoning.

Discussion Question(s)

1. What good have you seen in the delaying of gifts from Allah سبحانه وتعالى؟

110. Ayesha's To-Do List

Between Fajr and Dhuhr, Ayesha had done the following:

i.   Gone for a jog

ii.   Took a shower

iii.   Got dressed

iv.   Ate breakfast

v.   Played with her baby sister

After Dhuhr, she exclaimed to herself: "*Alhamdulillah* {thanks to Allah سبحانه وتعالى}, who allowed me to spend the whole morning in His worship!"

In practice...

Intention is crucial in everything we do [10]. There are permissible activities in religion, such as eating, having fun, sleeping, etc. We can turn these permissible activities into worship if we have an intention to do so. We may say, "I am eating so that I can worship better," "I am taking a break from worship by having some fun so that I can concentrate and focus on my prayer once I return," etc. According to the Islamic tradition, the time and effort spent in these regular actions can transform into worship and will be pleasing to Allah سبحانه وتعالى.

Discussion Question(s)

1. Can intentions ever have a bad effect on actions?

111. Ya-Wahid, Ya-Ahad!

As Ghuydar goes about his day, he would often bring his heart to remember Allah سبحانه وتعالى as a way of maintaining focus through the vicissitudes of life. *"Ya-Wahid,"* he would invoke as he went about his daily activities. As the day winds down and he reaches home, he would dedicate some time to remember his Lord with full focus. *"Ya-Ahad"*, he would now invoke, as he called onto his Creator.

.

In practice...

It is important to be with Allah سبحانه وتعالى in our minds and hearts. *Al Wahid* means "Allah سبحانه وتعالى, The One, The Creator of Diversity from Unity," while *Al-Ahad* means "Allah سبحانه وتعالى, The One and Only, The Unity, The Sole One". Sometimes, the distractions in life can make us heedless of Allah سبحانه وتعالى. With constant effort and struggle, it is important to connect to the attributes of *Al-Wahid* and *Al-Ahad*.

Discussion Question(s)

1. What are the benefits of learning the different names/attributes of Allah سبحانه وتعالى?

112. A Different Kind of treat

To say that Mariam loved baklawa would be an understatement. Any opportunity she had to eat the delicious treat was seized without question. And if there was ever such a chance, it would be the day of Eid-ul-Fitr. However, this past Eid was unique. After 30 days of fasting, reading the Quran and praying Salah, Mariam was feeling…to say the least…different. Although, she had been Muslim her whole life, this was the first time she was really tasting faith. And it was sweet. Her belief during the holy month had a "realness" she had never felt. After the khutbah on Eid day, she hugged fellow sisters in the prayer rows and wished them a happy Eid. After what felt like dozens of embraces, she came across her good friend, Ayesha. And lo and behold, she saw it: A large table covered with refreshments and tucked in the middle, lay a large dish of the self-indulging dessert. Indeed, it was a baklawa bonanza. This was Mariam's moment of truth. After some internal struggles, she turned away from the table, grabbed Ayesha by the arms and pulled her towards the mosque parking lot. "A healthy breakfast sounds great for this Eid," Mariam told her friend. A surprised Ayesha protested and responded, "But what about the baklawa?" Mariam smiled and remarked: "I have a different type of treat that I am saving for later".

In practice...

It is important to be aware and mindful of what one eats [15]. We should eat pure, healthy, and blessed foods. Keeping the body healthy can make it easier for us to build and sustain our connection with Allah سبحانه وتعالى. It is also important to have the intention and goal of having a long healthy life in this world in order to prolong the sweetness of worship and relationship with Allah سبحانه وتعالى.

Discussion Question(s)

1. What do you do if you are not feeling the sweetness of worship? Is it essential to feel something while worshipping Allah سبحانه وتعالى؟

Glossary

Accountability: liability, especially in Sufism and in Abrahamic traditions; everyone has a free will in this world but will be accountable for his (her) actions in the afterlife before Allah سبحانه وتعالى.

Adab: etiquette, good manners, esp. in the relationship with Allah سبحانه وتعالى

Affair: relationship

Alhamdulillah: a recited divine phrase of appreciation to Allah سبحانه وتعالى

Alienating: isolating, separating, disconnecting

Allah: proper name of Allah سبحانه وتعالى in Islam

Anger: uncontrolled and chaotic human spiritual state

Arabic: language, especially the language of revelation of the Quran

Arrogance: feelings and actions of superiority

Assert: claim

Astagfirullah: a divine phrase of asking forgiveness from Allah سبحانه وتعالى and cleansing the heart

Authentic: original, genuine, true

Balance: modesty, especially in Sufism, following the middle course

Bismillah: a divine phrase of starting something with the blessing of Allah سبحانه وتعالى

Chanting or *Dhikr*: repeating, especially in Sufism, repeating the phrases with focus and experience

Conscience: internal instinct of distinguishing between right or wrong

Constant: not changing, permanent

Construction: formation of an abstract entity

Death: end of a person's physical faculties

Dedication: sincere and constant effort

Deity: representation of the transcendent

Discharge: negative states of spirituality that makes a person sad, stressed, or anxious

Divine: transcendent

Dominance: control

Dream: visions when one is sleeping or awake

Ego: self, identifier of a person, especially in Islam

Embodiment: making it part of one's character

Endeavor: engagement, activities

Ethical: moral

Etiquette: adab, good manners and respect, especially in the relationship with Allah سبحانه وتعالى

Evil: anything that causes stress, sadness, or anxiety

Experience or experiential knowledge: all types of learning, except from a teacher or text,; internalizing and personalizing the formal learning

Genuine: sincere, original, authentic

Glorification: the mental, spiritual, and verbal acts of describing Allah سبحانه وتعالى in an admirable way

Heaven: a place of all maximized pleasures of bodily and spiritual engagements while being with Allah سبحانه وتعالى

Humility: character or trait of modesty

Illa Allah: except Allah سبحانه وتعالى

InshAllah: Allah سبحانه وتعالى willing, hopefully

Intention: planning ideas before the action

Internalize: making it part of one's character, trait, or nature

Islam: name of a religion that emphasizes belief in one Creator (Allah سبحانه وتعالى), belief in Jesus, Moses, and Muhammad as human prophets of the Creator

Jihad: struggle, esp. spiritual struggle within oneself

Journey: struggles of following guidelines of a mystical school

Knowledge: theoretical understanding of something through education

La ilaha illa Allah: there is no Allah سبحانه وتعالى except Allah, a critical Divine phrase of *Dhikr* in Islam

Lord: Allah سبحانه وتعالى

Meditation: deep focus, especially with reflection

Mercy: compassion and forgiveness

Mind: logic, reason, and rationality

Miracle: an effect or extraordinary event in the physical world that surpasses all known human explanations and reasoning

Mosque: place of worship for Muslims

Muhammad: the last Prophet of Islam, referred as "the Prophet ﷺ" in the text.

Mystic: a person who adopts the teachings of mysticism

Mysticism: the knowledge of the transcendent

Nafs: self in its raw form

Notion: concept, idea

Odd: not even, unique, no equivalence

One: denoting the one and only Creator

Oppression: unjust action of the strong over the weak

Permanent: constant, not changing, not ending

Phenomenon: occurrence

Pious: devout, practicing

Popular culture: the ethnographic data gathered over the period of years among different communities

Quran: sacred and divine text of Muslims

Recitation: reading, to read

Reliance: dependence

Reward: prize, payment, especially in worldly and afterlife rewards in Islam

Saint: pious person who is believed to be close to Allah سبحانه وتعالى

Sakina: peaceful and calm feelings

Salawat: names of the *Dhikr* to remember teachers and their covenants with their students, especially the main teacher, the Prophet Muhammad and others, such as Abraham, Moses, and Jesus

Scholar: expert, especially in Sufism, the experts who practice what they teach (alim)

Self: ego, identifier of a person

Service: ethical action of doing good for others and society

Struggle: efforts to achieve a goal

SubhanAllah: glorification of Allah سبحانه وتعالى, a divine phrase of *Dhikr* of spirituality implying a spiritual charge and discharge

Submission: natural acceptance of the uncontrolled and unseen

Sufi: follower of Sufism

Sufism: mystical path of Islam

Surrender: involuntary state of acceptance of the uncontrolled and the unseen

Taqwa: respect of Allah سبحانه وتعالى

Taste: pleasure, especially spiritual pleasure such as peace, calmness, joy, and happiness

The Divine: Allah سبحانه وتعالى

The Prophet ﷺ: Muhammad, the last Prophet ﷺ of Islam

Trait: permanent character or nature

Tranquility: peace and calmness

Transcendent: beyond human limits

Transitory: temporal

Transliteration: writing the sounds of words or phrases from one language to another

Unseen: anything the five human senses cannot observe

Weak: not having the physical or spiritual strength to perform an action

Worshipper: a person who regularly follows and practices rituals, acts of prayers

Suggested Readings

Al-Ghazali, M. *Deliverance from Error.* Fons Vitae, 2000.

Al-Ghazali, M. *Ihya 'Ulum al-Din.'* Dar al-Fikr, 2004.

Al-Ghazzali, M. *On the Treatment of Anger, Hatred and Envy.* Kazi Publications, 2003.

Al-Ghazzali, M. *e Alchemy of Happiness.* Routledge, 2015.

Ali, A. Y. *e Meaning of the Glorious Quran.* Islamic Books, 1938.

Anjum, Z. Iqbal: *e Life of a Poet, Philosopher, and Politician.* Random House, 2015.

Arberry, A. *Interpretation of Koran.* Macmillan, 1955.

Arberry. *Muslim Saints and Mystics: Episodes from Tadhirat al awliya of Faird al-Din Attar, Omphaloskepsis*, 2000.

Asad, M. *e Message of the Quran: Translated and Explained.* Al-Andalus Gibraltar, 1980.

Avery, K. S. *A Psychology of Early Su Sama: Listening and Altered States.* Routledge, 2004.

Awang, R. "Anger Management: A Psychotherapy Sufistic Approach," vol. 9, no. 1, 2014, pp. 13–15.

Barks, C. *Rumi: Bridge to the Soul.* Harperone, 2007.

Barks, R. N. C. and J. Moyne, *Rumi, Jelaluddin. "guest house." Essential Rumi.* Harper, 1995, p. 109.

Bayrak, T. *Name & the Named.* Canada, 2000.

Berguno, G. & Loutfy, N. "Existential Thoughts of the Su s. Existential Analysis." *Journal of the Society for Existential Analysis*, vol. 16, no. 1, 2005.

Bowen, J. *A New Anthropology of Islam.* Cambridge University Press, 2012.

Clarke, M. "Cough Sweets and Angels: Ordinary Ethics of the Extraordinary in Sufi Practice in Lebanon." *Journal of the Royal Anthropological Institute*, vol. 20, no. 3, 2014, pp. 407–25.

Cutsinger, J. S. *Paths to the Heart.* World Wisdom, 2010. Douglas-Klotz, N. *e Su Book of Life: 99 Pathways of the Heart for the Modern Dervish.* Penguin, 2005.

Ernst, C. W. *Teachings of Sufism.* Shambhala Publications, 1999.

Esposito, J. *e Oxford Dictionary of Islam.* Oxford University Press, 2014.

Friedlander, S. *e Whirling Dervishes: Being an Account of the Sufi Order Known as the Mevlevis and its Founder the Poet and Mystic Mevlana Jalalu'ddin Rumi.* SUNY Press, 1975.

Geoffroy, E. *Introduction to Sufism: Inner Path of Islam.* World Wisdom, Inc., 2010.

Gibran, K. *e Prophet.* Oneworld Publications, 2012.

Hanson, Y. H. "Creed of Imam Al-Tahawi." Zaytuna Institute, California, 2007.

Hanson, Y. H. *Purification of the Heart.* Alhambra Productions, 1998.

Helminski, K. *The Knowing Heart: A Sufi Path of Transformation.* Shambhala Publications, 2000.

Izutsu, T. *Sufism and Taoism: A Comparative Study of Key Philosophical Concepts.* University of California Press, 2016.

James, W. "Will to Believe." *New World*, 1896.

Jawziyyah, Q. *e Prophetic Medical Science.* Idara Impex, 2013.

Karamustafa, T. A. *Su sm.* Edinburgh University Press, 2007.

Katz, J. G. "Dreams, Sufism, and Sainthood." *Brill,* vol. 71, 1996.

Khan, Z. M. *Gardens of the Righteous.* Routledge, 2012.

Lewis, B. *Music of a Distant Drum: Classical Arabic, Persian, Turkish,and Hebrew Poems.* Princeton University Press, 2001.

Malak, A. *Muslim Narratives and the Discourse of English.* SUNY Press, 2007.

Morris, J. W. "Introducing Ibn 'Arabī's Book of Spiritual Advice." *Journal of the Muhyiddīn Ibn 'Arabī Society,* no. 28, 2000, pp. 1–17.

Pickthall, M. W. E. *Holy Quran.* Kutub Khana Isha'at-ul-Islam, 1977.

Ramji, R. *Global Migration of Su Islam to South Asia and Beyond.* Brill, 2007, pp. 473–84.

Renard J. *Knowledge of Allah سبحانه وتعالى in Classical Sufism: Foundations of Islamic Mystical Theology.* Paulist Press, 2004.

Rumi, J. *e Essential Rumi.* Harper, 1996.

Schimmel, A. *Deciphering the Signs of Allah سبحانه وتعالى: A Phenomenological Approach to Islam.* State University of New York Press, 1994.

Siddiqui, A. "Sahih Muslim." *Peace Vision,* 1972.

Trimingham, J. S. *Sufi Orders in Islam.* Oxford University Press, 1998.

Upton, C. *Doorkeeper of the Heart: Versions of Rabi'a.* Threshold Books, 1988.

Usmani, T. *An Approach to the Quranic Sciences.* Adam Publishers, 2006.

Index

Bibliography

[1] A. Salamah-Qudsi, Sufism and Early Islamic Piety: Personal and Communal Dynamics, Cambridge University Press, 2018.

[2] A. Muslim, Sahih Muslim (translated by Siddiqui, A.), Peace Vision, 1972.

[3] A. B. Hanbal, Musnad Imam Ahmad Ibn Hanbal, Dar-Us-Salam Publications, 2012.

[4] Y. J. Kumek, Practical Mysticism: Sufi Journeys of Heart and Mind, Dubuque: Kendall Hunt, 2018.

[5] A. Ansar, Peace of Mind and Healing Broken Lives, Universal Mercy, 2010.

[6] J. I. S. a. Y. Y. Haddad, The Islamic Understanding of Death and Resurrection, Oxford University Press, 2002.

[7] J. L. S. Dorothy G. Singer, Handbook of Children and the Media, SAGE, 2002.

[8] N. C. Ring, Introduction to the Study of Religion, New York: Orbis, 2007.

[9] T. Y. Ozkan, A Muslim Response to Evil: S. N. on the Theodicy, Routledge, 2016.

[10] M. Al-Bukhari, The translation of the meanings of Sahih Al-Bukhari, Kazi Publications, 1986.

[11] A. B. Al-Ansari, "Ahadith al-Shuyukh al-Thiqat," vol. 2, no. 322, pp. 875-876.

[12] G. Tamer, Islam and Rationality: The Impact of al-Ghazālī. Papers Collected on His 900th Anniversary, BRILL, 2015.

[13] E. Geoffroy, Introduction to Sufism: The Inner Path of Islam, World Wisdom, 2010.

[14] I. Shah, The Sufis, Octagon Press Ltd, 1999.

[15] A. J. &. N. Qubein, Life Balance The Sufi Way, Jaico Publishing House, 2007.

[16] I. Shah, Learning how to Learn: Psychology and Spirituality in the Sufi Way, Octagon Press Ltd,, 1978.

[17] K. L. H. Nicholas Heer, Three Early Sufi Texts, Fons Vitae, 2003.

[18] D. E. Singh, Sainthood and Revelatory Discourse: An Examination of the Bases for the Authority of Bayān in Mahwī Islam, David Emmanuel Singh, 2003.

[19] I. Darimi, Sunan Darimi, Beirut: Dar Al Kitab, 1997.

[20] M. I. I. Bukhari, Moral Teachings of Islam: Prophetic Traditions from Al-Adab Al-mufrad, Rowman Altamira, 2003.

[21] A. Schimmel, Deciphering the signs of Allah سبحانه وتعالى: a phenomenological approach to Islam., State Univ of New York Pr., 1994.

[22] B. F. Stowasser, The Day Begins at Sunset: Perceptions of Time in the Islamic World, I.B.Tauris, 2014.

[23] S. B. W. Al-Qahtani, Fortress Of Muslim, Darussalam Publishers, 2018.

[24] A. (. b. A. Dawud, Sunan Abu Dawud, Riyadh: Darussalam, 2008.

[25] A. Al-Qushayri, Al-Qushayri's Epistle on Sufism: Al-Risala Al-qushayriyya Fi 'ilm Al-tasawwu, Garnet & Ithaca Press, 2007.

[26] I. K. Ibn Qayyim, The Soul's Journey After Death, Noah, 2018.

[27] M. A. Khan, Encyclopaedia of Sufism: Sufism and Naqshbandi order, Anmol Publications, 2003.

[28] Adonis, Sufism and Surrealism, Saqi, 2013.

[29] B. Muhaiyaddeen, Dhikr: The Remembrance of Allah سبحانه وتعالى, Fellowship Press, 1999.

[30] P. M. Abdullah, ISLAMIC TASAWWUF : Shariah And Tariqah, Adam Publishers & Distributors, 2001.

[31] L. Vaughan-Lee, Love is a Fire: The Sufi's Mystical Journey Home, The Golden Sufi Center, 2000.

[32] M. Tirmizi, Jami At-Tirmizi, Dar-us-Salam, 2007.

[33] M. Tirmizi, Jami At-Tirmizi, Salat 13 (171).

[34] A. (. b. A. Dawud, Sunan Abu Dawud, riyadh: Darussalam, 2008.

[35] A. An-Nasa'i, Sunan An-Nasai, Riyadh: Daraussalalm, 2007.

[36] J. B., Interviewee, *Anthropologial Field Notes with New Comers.* [Interview]. 11 June 2007.

[37] Y. Kumek, Selected Passages from the Quran, Dubuque, Iowa: KendalHunt, 2018, p. 67.

[38] I. Majah, Sunan Ibn Majah, Darus-Salam, 2007.

---

[i] The experiential knowledge is critical. One can review Rumi's famous dialogue with his teacher about the importance of experiential knowledge.
[ii] The expression "spoiling the honey" comes from the statement of the Prophet Muhammad ﷺ that anger spoils the faith.
[iii] [49:13]

iv [39, 42]

v [41, 21]

vi [49:2]

vii [94, 1-8]

viii [3,159]

www.ingramcontent.com/pod-product-compliance
Lightning Source LLC
Chambersburg PA
CBHW032118040426
42449CB00005B/187